ARIZONA
MYTHS & LEGENDS

LEGENDS OF THE WEST SERIES

ARIZONA
MYTHS & LEGENDS

THE TRUE STORIES BEHIND
HISTORY'S MYSTERIES

SECOND EDITION

SAM LOWE

TWODOT®

GUILFORD, CONNECTICUT
HELENA, MONTANA

A · TWODOT® · BOOK

An imprint of Rowman & Littlefield

Distributed by NATIONAL BOOK NETWORK

British Library Cataloguing-in-Publication Information available

Library of Congress Cataloging-in-Publication Data available

ISBN 978-1-4930-2304-2 (paperback)
ISBN 978-1-4930-2305-9 (e-book)

∞™ The paper used in this publication meets the minimum requirements of American National Standard for Information Sciences—Permanence of Paper for Printed Library Materials, ANSI/NISO Z39.48-1992.

CONTENTS

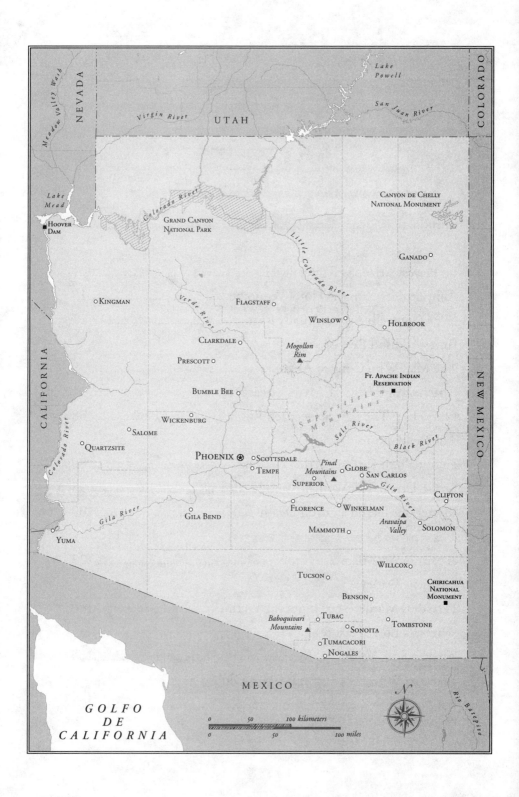

CONTENTS

INTRODUCTION

First, a matter of clarification: This is not intended to be a reference book. Rather, it is a collection of stories based on fact. It also includes, however, large doses of supposition, suggestion, hearsay, secondhand information, folklore, saloon and barroom recollections, old wives' tales, speculation, and even a smattering of outright fibbing. But quite naturally, all of these are vital content in a publication dealing with myths, mysteries, and legends, which this one does.

I gathered the information from newspaper clippings, magazine articles, websites, reference books, autobiographies, and personal interviews, so it is as factual as I could make it. But regardless of my efforts, it was inevitable that some of those aforementioned elements would slip into my accounts. And, I must admit, I gleefully included them.

The people mentioned herein are long since departed, but their stories live on, usually through books like this. And through supposition, suggestions, hearsay, secondhand information, folklore, saloon and barroom recollections, old wives' tales, speculation, and fibs.

So read it with that understanding.

And, of course, enjoy.

IRA HAYES:
ARIZONA'S RELUCTANT HERO

In the chill of the early morning hours of January 24, 1955, members of the Gila River Indian community found the body of one of their friends lying cold near a canal on a patch of desert near Bapchule, a small reservation town south of Phoenix. They recognized him immediately. It was Ira Hayes.

Ira Hayes.

An American legend, dead at such an early age.

A reluctant hero who became a sacrifice during the Second World War.

His tormented life was over. He was only thirty-two years old. But his last few years were a living hell, ignited by the horrors of combat and fueled by well-intended but misplaced homage. Now those who knew him best silently hoped that, in his death, he might find the peace that had eluded him for so many years.

The coroner's report listed alcohol and exposure as the major causes of death. It made no mention of either grief or torment, although these surely played a part.

History may record Ira Hamilton Hayes as a hero but, in his own eyes, he neither deserved nor wanted the designation. The government and the military promoted him as an idol and a

Ira Hayes made for a most reluctant war hero.

grateful America accepted him as one. Then once his time in the national spotlight was over, he became a victim, a man who never asked for public acclaim but had it thrust upon him.

And it ruined his life.

Ira Hayes was a Pima Indian first, then a marine, then an unwilling hero. The act that ushered him into a wholly unwanted lifestyle was a chance happening, not a brave deed. He just happened to be there when a single moment immortalized him. He was forced to go along for the ride, regardless of where it took him.

The events leading up to what would become his downfall began on February 19, 1945. American military forces invaded Iwo Jima, a small but strategic island in the South Pacific about seven hundred miles south of Tokyo, Japan. It was a possible supply point for the Allied forces, who considered it important that they prevent the Japanese from using it themselves. Hayes was a part of a landing team met with withering, never-ending fire from the Japanese forces who held the tiny piece of land. Four days later, on February 23, the invaders had captured enough ground to take control. The officers in charge ordered a flag-raising ceremony atop Mount Suribachi, the highest point on the island at 516 feet above sea level.

But the flag they hoisted was deemed too small by the higher-ups, so they gave the order for a second ceremony. This time, armed with a larger flag and accompanied by photographer Joe Rosenthal and about forty fellow servicemen, five marines and a navy corpsman hiked to the top of the peak and planted the second banner. Rosenthal, an Associated Press cameraman, snapped the picture. Days later, the photo appeared on the front pages of newspapers all across America. The act of raising the flag was hailed with all the plaudits that normally accompany great feats of heroism.

It was the first step along a path that would lead to tragedy for five of the six young servicemen shown in Rosenthal's photograph.

Three of the flag raisers—Sgt. Mike Strank of Pennsylvania, Cpl. Harlon Block of Texas, and Pvt. Franklin Sousley of Kentucky—died as the fighting continued on Iwo Jima. The other three were selected to tour the United States as spokesmen for war bond rallies. Each handled the assignment differently. John Bradley, the navy corpsman from Wisconsin, did his duty but then kept his role in the incident a secret, hiding it even from his family, who never knew about it until after his death in 1994. Pvt. Rene Gagnon of New Hampshire tried to capitalize on his fame but it led to business failures, divorce, and alcoholism, culminated by a premature death in 1979.

And Ira Hayes, the Pima Indian from Arizona, tried to run from it only to become a martyr.

Rosenthal's image (which shows Hayes at the far left) was awarded a Pulitzer Prize and eventually became the world's most reproduced photograph. The fight for Iwo Jima stands as the worst battle in Marine Corps history with more than twenty-two thousand casualties, more than they sustained during several months of battle at Guadalcanal.

Ira Hayes was not among them.

Not at first.

But he was most definitely a casualty.

These days, few people on the Gila River Indian Reservation remember the man behind the story. He was born on the reservation on January 12, 1923, and died there a little more than thirty-two years later. He was a member of the Pima tribe, the eldest of eight children. Although shy and introverted, he earned good grades at Sacaton and the Phoenix Indian School. He left high school after completing two years of study to serve in the Civilian Conservation Corps for a couple of months before taking a job as a carpenter. On August 26, 1942, he enlisted in the Marine Corps Reserve at Phoenix for a period referred to by the federal government as the "duration of the national emergency." After giving its approval, the tribe sent one of its sons off to fight. It was tradition, in a way. The Pimas had always been known as protectors.

After boot camp in San Diego, he was assigned to the Parachute Training School at Camp Gillespie, also in San Diego. He graduated a month later and was promoted to private first class. Because he was a Pima Indian, he also became known as "Chief Falling Cloud" among his fellow jumpers. At the time there were overtones of racial prejudice against Hayes and other Native Americans in the service. If the nickname bothered him, Hayes never spoke of it. There was a war going on, and he had a duty to perform.

In December 1942 he joined a parachute battalion at Camp Elliott in California and in March sailed with that unit for Nouméa, New Caledonia. The following October, the battalion saw combat at Vella Lavella in the Solomon Islands, then moved north to Bougainville where a campaign was already under way. The parachutists saw considerable action before leaving in January 1944. Hayes was ordered back to San Diego a month later. With his parachute unit disbanded, he was transferred to Company E, Second Battalion, Twenty-eighth Marines, of the Fifth Marine Division at

Camp Pendleton. The company was sent to Hawaii for more training, then shipped to Iwo Jima for the attack that would eventually lead Hayes to his ill-fated encounter with fame.

He fought on the island for thirty-six days and came out of the battle unscathed. Yet when the war over and all the ensuing furor came to an end, he returned to his homeland and told his friends that he felt a deep sense of guilt because he survived the assault on Iwo Jima while so many of his comrades didn't.

And it also disturbed him that the incident which raised him to the rank of hero was something he considered minor and relatively unimportant. But the nation that elevated him to that status saw it differently.

Rosenthal's photograph restored the faith of a war-weary America and became the centerpiece for a huge fund-raising drive. The War Department needed heroes and the Treasury Department needed money. Hayes, Gagnon, and Bradley were selected to fill both needs. They were taken out of their unit and sent on a national tour that eventually produced two billion dollars for the war effort. The three young men were proclaimed heroes by the entire nation and drinking buddies by many of their admirers. Hayes, a nondrinker until then, was too polite to refuse when an extended hand usually held an alcoholic beverage.

So he drank and made polite talk because he was a marine and it was his duty. But beneath this thin veneer, there was a shy young man who simply wished to be left alone. "He was a reluctant hero," distant cousin Sara Bernal told the *Arizona Republic* in a 1998 interview. "The attention thrust upon him played a big part in his early death."

The illustrious trio appeared at bond rallies and portrayed themselves, although very briefly, in *Sands of Iwo Jima*, a war movie that starred John Wayne. They were brought in as actor/consultants but were on the screen for just a few minutes, were rarely asked for advice, and eventually realized they were being used by the producers to market the film because of their nationwide appeal. They also met celebrities and visited the White House, where President Harry Truman called Hayes "a great American hero." But the adulation only embarrassed Hayes.

"It was supposed to be soft duty," he later told an interviewer, "but I couldn't take it. Everywhere we went, people shoved drinks into our hands and said, 'You're a hero!' We knew we hadn't done that much, but you couldn't tell them that."

And in another interview, he said, "How could I feel like a hero when only five men in my platoon of 45 survived, when only 27 men in my company of 250 managed to escape death or injury?"

The tour continued anyway. The men were sent on a thirty-two-city junket, and a million and a half people cheered them in Times Square. The press put them on a pedestal; the public wouldn't let them down. In his book *Flags of Our Fathers*, author James Bradley (flag-raiser John Bradley's son) wrote, "Ira, in particular, couldn't compute. It was a Beatlemania-like tour and every handclasp was like a knife in his heart because he felt like he was living a lie."

The bright lights, the hero worship, and the glad-handing began to take a toll. Hayes started drinking heavily and was removed from the bond tour in Chicago and sent back to the Twenty-eighth Marines at Hilo, Hawaii. Three weeks later, he was promoted to corporal. At the end of the war, Hayes and his company were shipped to Sasebo, Japan, where they participated in the occupation of the defeated country. On October 25, 1945, he boarded ship for the eleventh time and returned to the United States, landing at San Francisco, where he was honorably discharged on December 1, 1945.

During his military career, Hayes was awarded a Letter of Commendation with Commendation Ribbon by Lt. Gen. Roy S. Geiger, the commanding general of the Pacific Fleet Marine Force, for his "meritorious and efficient performance of duty while serving with a marine infantry battalion during operations against the enemy on Vella Lavella and Bougainville . . . and on Iwo Jima."

He also received a Navy Commendation Ribbon with "V" Combat Device, Presidential Unit Citation with one star (for Iwo Jima), Asiatic-Pacific Campaign Medal with four stars, American Campaign Medal, and the World War II Victory Medal.

After his discharge, Hayes returned to his home and tried to return to the life he had known before 1942. In his vain attempt to regain anonymity, he turned more inward than ever, keeping the tortured thoughts about what he had seen and done during the war locked inside. But fame held him in an unyielding grip. People drove out to the reservation to shake his hand and have their pictures taken with him. Then they told other people, and the other people repeated the scenario until Hayes was forced to leave home because it was his only hope of finding solitude. "I kept getting hundreds of letters," he told friends. "And people would drive through the reservation, walk up to me and ask, 'Are you the Indian who raised the flag on Iwo Jima?'"

With help from a relocation program sponsored by the Bureau of Indian Affairs, he went to Chicago and found a job as an assistant lathe operator with International Harvester Company. It removed him from the public eye, but the respite was only temporary. Once his employers found out who he was, they exploited him in their company magazine with an article entitled "Hero in Our Midst," which also included his Chicago address. Then came the inevitable. Once the public knew who he was and where he was, they wanted to meet a hero. The phone calls were endless, both day and night, and people pounded on the door of his apartment, demanding that they be allowed to speak with him. The pressure grew; so did his drinking problem. Within three weeks after the article appeared, the police picked him up in a skid row area of the Loop at 1:00 a.m. He was staggering, his shirt was torn, and he was not wearing shoes. He was sent to jail.

This time, help came from an unusual source. The *Chicago Sun-Times* also discovered who he was, got him out of jail, and started a fund-raiser to help with his rehabilitation. That led to a job in Los Angeles, where everyone involved hoped he could make a fresh start and forget the reason for his situation. Hayes was grateful, and said he was "cured of drinking." But the cure lasted less than a week. He was arrested by Los Angeles police on the familiar charge of public drunkenness.

"I was sick," he told his family and friends. "I guess I was about to crack up, thinking about all my good buddies. They were better men than me and they're not coming back, much less back to the White House, like me."

Frustrated at both himself and the circumstances that surrounded him, Hayes returned to the reservation once more. But this time there was no hero's welcome and only one reporter took the time to interview the fallen idol. He was despondent and appeared to have given up on himself. "I guess I'm just no good," he told the reporter. "I've had a lot of chances, but just when things started looking good, I get that craving for whisky and foul up." He thought that going back to his family might help.

In the meantime, Rene Gagnon became the darling of the media. He had carried the flag up Mount Suribachi, was the youngest survivor of the episode, and willingly cooperated with interviewers. So his handsome face helped sell a lot of newspapers. But the same media that made him a hero later turned on him, producing lurid stories about his problems.

John Bradley, the navy corpsman, avoided all the heartbreak by remaining silent. He told his fiancée about it only once, on their second date. The couple raised a family that never knew of his involvement until James Bradley started digging into his father's past prior to writing his book.

And Ira's downward spiral continued. He was arrested fifty-five times on drunkenness charges and could find neither work nor peace. He returned to the spotlight infrequently. The first time was in 1950 when he went to Washington to plead for more assistance for his tribe. There was another momentary break in his torment in 1954 when he was invited back to Washington to attend the dedication of the Iwo Jima Memorial. During the ceremony, President Dwight Eisenhower lauded him as a hero. Afterwards, a reporter asked how he liked all the pomp and circumstance that goes with being a famous person. "I don't," was his only reply.

Three months later, he was dead.

An editorial in the *Phoenix Gazette* on January 26, 1954, declared: "Ira Hayes was a victim of war as surely as though he had died on Iwo Jima with his buddies. The peace he fought to win never brought him personal peace. But he is no less a hero for that. Arizona will always honor his memory and the proud symbol he helped create."

However, not even death could bring about the solitude he pursued so vainly. State lawmakers decided he should get a state funeral. Thousands of Arizonans paid respects as his body lay in state in the state capitol before his burial in Arlington National Cemetery.

In 1960 Hollywood stepped in to convert a reluctant hero into a larger-than-life hero by casting Lee Marvin as Hayes in a telefilm entitled *The American*. A year later, Tony Curtis portrayed Hayes as a man destined to become a tribal leader in a full-length film, *The Outsider*. The movie was based on a segment of *Wolf Whistle and Other Stories*, a collection written by William Bradford Huie. In that selection, also called "The Outsider," Huie was the first to recount Hayes's reactions to his unwanted fame. Years later, in the 2006 movie *Flags of Our Fathers*, based on James Bradley's book and directed by Clint Eastwood, Adam Beach appears as Hayes.

Songwriter Peter La Farge and country singer Johnny Cash also added misguided laurels. La Farge wrote "The Ballad of Ira

Hayes" and Cash recorded it in 1963. It went to third place on the music charts. The refrain called him "drunken Ira Hayes" and referred to him as a "whisky drinkin' Indian."

However, in an interview conducted shortly before his book was published, Bradley noted: "I've spoken to many of Ira's Marine buddies who fought with him, who shared foxholes with him and who depended upon Ira for their lives. They don't talk about an out-of-control guy or a drunk. No, when these veterans speak of Ira, they do so with respect and tell of an honorable warrior. And that is what killed Ira Hayes. A conflict of honor."

Bradley also presented some reliable evidence that Hayes was more than likely suffering from post-traumatic stress disorder. The affliction is common today but did not receive major attention until the 1960s, much too late to help Ira Hayes.

Typically, many kind words were spoken about him after his death. At his funeral, Gagnon eulogized, "Let's say he had a little dream in his heart that someday the Indian would be like the white man [and] be able to walk all over the United States."

And on November 10, 1993, in a speech delivered at the Iwo Jima Memorial, Marine Corps Commandant Gen. Carl Mundy declared:

One of the pairs of hands that you see outstretched to raise our national flag on the battle-scarred crest of Mount Suribachi so many years ago are those of a Native American, Ira Hayes, a Marine not of the ethnic majority of our population. Were Ira Hayes here today, I would tell him that although my words on another occasion have given the impression that I believe some Marines, because of their color, are not as capable as other Marines, that those were not the thoughts of my mind and that they are not the thoughts of my heart.

I would tell Ira Hayes that our Corps is what we are because we are the people of America . . . the people of the broad, strong, ethnic fabric that is our nation. And last, I would tell him that in the future, that our fabric will broaden and strengthen in every category to make our Corps even stronger, even of greater utility to our nation. That's a commitment of this commandant, and that's a personal commitment of this Marine.

Today in Sacaton, where he was born, a memorial park features a life-size bronze of Ira Hayes, dressed in his marine uniform and wearing what might best be construed as a look of peace, standing in front of a plaque bearing a bas-relief of the flag raising on Iwo Jima. And in Bapchule, where he received his early education, Ira Hayes High School stands as the only upper-level school on the Gila River Reservation.

In Arlington National Cemetery, his remains lie in Section 34, Plot 479A. And the huge Iwo Jima Memorial is a never-changing reminder of an incident that gave a nation hope during a tragic time in history. Two days after Rosenthal's photograph appeared, lawmakers rose from the floor of the Senate to call for a national monument honoring the flag raising. State legislators passed similar resolutions and thousands of Americans wrote to President Truman, urging him to act in a hurry.

Ira Hayes is memorialized in bronze in a park in Sacaton.

A mere seventy-two hours after seeing the photograph, artist Felix DeWeldon sculpted a clay replica of the picture and brought it to the White House. Truman approved and gave the order to start the design and creation process. Hundreds of artisans worked on the project, and Hayes, Gagnon, and Bradley were all brought in to pose for their figures. The artists used photographs and measurements to re-create the images of Strank, Block, and Sousley. The work was dedicated on November 10, 1954. The figures of the six men stand thirty-two feet tall, and the flagpole rises sixty feet.

And just as he was on February 23, 1945, Ira Hayes is the marine at the far left.

ABBY STILL LIVES IN THE HOTEL VENDOME

The Hotel Vendome in Prescott is one of those places that invites strangers in, shows them to a comfortable chair, then surrounds them with a sense of longing for bygone times. It is a wonderful old building situated in a wonderful old neighborhood dotted with wonderful old Victorian houses. The narrow streets are lined with wonderful old trees and the cars park diagonally like they used to when life was, according to those who were there at the time, less stressful and more relaxed than it is now.

The structure is two stories, flat roofed, made of brick, and it runs from the street clear back to the alley. A veranda stretches across the front on both levels. Guests on either floor can pull up a chair or prop their feet on the white railings, then sit and watch the world wander by.

Guests also have the option of a delightful tête-à-tête in the hotel lobby, where a small wine bar dispenses clarets and ports while the guests pore over scrapbooks filled with clippings and testimonials about Abby and Noble, the resident ghosts. (For those who prefer their spirits in liquid form, Prescott's infamous Whiskey Row is within easy walking distance. The block-long assortment of bars and eateries has a colorful history and associated tall tales that

SAM LOWE PHOTO

Some guests at the Hotel Vendome in Prescott claim to witness strange occurrences.

still attract tourists, gawkers, and those interested in nightlife of a more tangible kind.)

The front desk in the lobby of the Hotel Vendome is small and sturdy. There's an antique wooden key case on the wall, and the guests who register there can look directly down a long hallway to the first-floor rooms, or glance to their right where a wooden staircase will take them to the upper level.

To Room 16, where Abby and Noble supposedly hang out.

According to local legend, the two have been living rent free in the Hotel Vendome for more than ninety years. Abby was an abandoned wife; Noble was her cat. The oft-told story is that around 1920, Abby Bry and her husband (whose name is never mentioned) owned the hotel, but they fell upon hard times and had to sell out. Fortunately, the new owners liked the couple and let them stay on as caretakers. They were allowed to live in Room 16, but they didn't live happily ever after.

One reason for the compassion shown the pair is that Abby suffered from tuberculosis. Her life was slowly ebbing away because of the affliction, which was then commonly known as "consumption." On a fateful night in 1921, Abby's life took an even more tragic turn when her husband went out for either medicine or cigarettes (the details are obscure even after years of research) and never returned.

Unable to deal with both her illness and abandonment, Abby went to bed and never got up again. She refused all offers of food, medicine, and consolation and, after a short period of self-imposed incarceration, died in February 1921 at the age of thirty-three. According to the legend, Noble remained faithfully at Abby's side during her final ordeal and perished at almost the same time.

And now the two roam the hallways, confusing the guests and sometimes even disturbing them. They make their presence known in a variety of ways. Some guests report actual encounters; others sense there's somebody or something in the room with them; and some say they smell the fragrance of roses.

Frank Langford, a former operator of the hotel along with his wife, Kathie, viewed all this with a degree of skepticism. He said he'd like to believe, but needed more concrete evidence.

"I walk the fence," he said one morning. "I believe in ghosts but I want to be convinced. I believe in God, the devil, afterlife, and angels. I can't see them, but that doesn't mean I don't believe in them."

He paused for a moment, then added, "At the same time, I don't see any actual signs of ghosts. I'd like to see an apparition."

Others aren't so reluctant to firmly state their belief that Abby exists. Not only does she exist, they say, but she wants people to know about her.

And the people respond in her favor.

Many of their recollections are kept in a three-inch-thick scrapbook that is moved from the lobby to Room 16 and back, depending on who is doing the housecleaning. One former guest wrote anonymously:

My family and I were staying in the Vendome hotel in Prescott. I knew it was haunted and that was the main reason I wanted to stay there. I was in the room I shared with my brother, watching television, and my family was all out on the porch talking. Suddenly, the room became deathly cold. I put on my thick jacket and I was still freezing. This would not have bothered me so much if it had not been in the middle of the day, and seconds before it had been warm.

After a minute or two, the door which I had pushed all the way closed kept on flying open. I went outside and closed it and no matter how hard I pushed, it did not open. I went in and asked my family if they had come inside recently and they said "no."

Later that night I went to sleep fairly easily but something or someone woke me up. I was half asleep but I remember someone talking to me. I am a very deep sleeper.

I checked and all my family was asleep. Just as I climbed into bed, the bell from down the street struck twelve. I have never been so afraid in my life.

Langford heard all these stories, and he related some of them after opening the door to Room 16. "Sometimes guests say they wake up to a perfume smell," he said. "It's definitely there, they say. They lie there and wait for something else but it's only a smell and then it's gone. I've had that happen to me. It gives me the chills."

Room 16 is small, very neat, and bears a strong resemblance to the room set aside for guests at Grandma's house. Lace curtains drift gently as a morning breeze courses its way across the quilted bedspread. A wicker chair sits next to the bed, and a wooden dresser stands guard at the foot. A transom tops the five-paneled wooden door. The only marked deviation from the style of the 1920s is the television set on top of the dresser.

There's a second door in the room. It opens into a closet, empty except for a long purple dress that hangs forlornly off a circular bar. A full-length mirror is attached to the inside of the door. Visitors open the door cautiously because earlier guests have written that they've seen a wispy figure reflected in the mirror.

The closet has significance, Langford said, because guests report a lot of unexplained activity there. Possible explanations include the story that Noble, the cat, was found hanging in the closet after Abby's death. Another tale says a young boy killed the cat then hid its body in the closet. And a third version has it that the boy killed the cat and then buried it behind the hotel.

But Langford also said Abby and Noble may not be the only ghosts in the hotel. "There are allegedly several other spirits here," he said. "They are not scary or evil. They're more like an overload of the senses. Things like chills, sensations of touch or pressure, like someone sitting on the edge of the bed. Fragrances and noises. Some are probably explainable, but when they become difficult to explain, they're chalked up as ghosts."

Later, he admitted that he had actually been involved in a couple of incidents that made him doubt his doubts.

"My closest encounter happened one day when I saw someone walk into Room 16," he said. "I just saw the person out of the corner of my eye. I'm not sure what it was but it looked like a female wearing a white blouse and black skirt, and she had dark hair. I went into the room to make sure somebody wasn't using it for a séance, or maybe using the bathroom, but there was no one there."

A Phoenix woman purposely stayed in the room. She didn't believe in ghosts but secretly wanted to see one. She later wrote in the scrapbook that "the bathroom light flickered off and on, the hangers in the closet moved back and forth and I distinctly heard a cat bell ringing." But even eerier, she wrote, was that as she watched from the bathroom door, the quilt on the unmade bed folded itself back up to the headboard.

Others claim they've seen Abby in detail. According to the stories they've written in the scrapbook, she is plain looking, medium height, auburn hair, and very busty. They also say she was a teacher, but history does not record Abby's occupation during her short life.

History, in fact, doesn't even record Abby herself. Prescott historians say they've combed all available documents from the 1920s and find no trace of either Abby or her husband. Their searches have taken them through city directories, census records, funeral registries, and cemetery records.

But they do know that the hotel was built in 1917 by J. B. Jones as an apartment house, and it was hailed at the time by the local press because it "will fill a need for housing in the town which was crucial even when the summer visitors were induced to return home."

According to the bronze plaque out front, the building is the only Prescott example of a two-story structure built exclusively for residential use during the first quarter of the twentieth century. It was initially advertised as "an attractive small hotel with 30 rooms and 16 baths, wide verandas upstairs and down, attractive lobby, hot and cold water in all rooms, night and day phone service with buzzers in all rooms, excellent steam heat, free parking, one-half block from the plaza, one block east of Highway 89, rates reasonable with $1.50 single and $2.50 double."

Cowboy movie actor Tom Mix rented a room by the year back in the 1920s, and the hotel is listed on the National Register of Historic Places. It was restored and modernized in 1983 and now features twenty-one rooms.

While he was in charge, Langford said he felt the hotel's history may also be involved with the alleged haunting. "Prior to its construction in 1917, a house stood here," he said. "Maybe some of the ghosts are lingering spirits from the house."

Abby's ghost still haunts Room 16 in the Hotel Vendome.

The old steam radiators definitely play a role. Although disconnected after the remodel in 1983, they were left in the rooms for ambience. But even today, some guests say, they rattle and clank like "someone hammering a request for the superintendent to turn up the heat."

Among the other ghostly doings are light switches that turn off and on by themselves, a meowing cat in the early hours, and incidents where the Do Not Disturb signs begin spinning around on the door knobs. "Perhaps there are some rational explanations for these things," Langford said, "but some just challenge logical explanation."

Kathie Langford reported two such instances on www.ghost corner.com, a now-defunct website for fans of the eerie and unexplained. In one case, four women said they all woke up at 3:00

a.m. to the smell of a strong, rose-scented perfume and a very cool breeze.

The other report said a man "walked out to the lobby at 3:00 a.m. to get a cup of coffee. Walking in the dimmed hall, back to his room, he became aware that his shadow was not in sync with his body movements. He stopped but the shadow continued down the hall and disappeared. He said he smelled perfume and a chill swept over him. He had not known the hotel was said to be haunted and said he did not believe in ghosts."

Some of the newspaper articles in the scrapbook quote current owner Rama Patel, who told reporters that some guests had seen Abby walking on the staircase and roaming the hallways. Sometimes the service bell on the registration desk rang when there was no one in the lobby, Patel said, and the front doorbell frequently rang when there was nobody there. Patel has owned the hotel for several years and assumed management in May 2009.

Guests have also claimed that the television sets work only when there's a Western movie being shown. One wrote that the set, which normally broadcasts in color, went to black-and-white during a science-fiction program about the paranormal, and stayed that way until the show ended.

A rather determined guest wrote that he had left a tape recorder running overnight in Room 16. He said he'd share the findings with the hotel staff but never produced any results. Others used a Ouija board to establish what they said was proof that Abby not only wanders the hallways but anywhere else in the hotel that she darn well pleases. Frank Langford gave partial credibility to that report.

"The sensations are mostly in Room 16 but are not confined to it," he said. "Rooms 19, 23, and 25 have also had sightings and other occurrences. So if they are spirits, they're wandering spirits. The parapsychologists who have examined the hotel say there's definitely a female presence here, but say there's also a male. It's a real mystery."

Several pages of the Abby scrapbook contain photographs taken in Room 16 and the adjacent hallways. Most of them don't show anything out of the ordinary, despite the claims of the photographers. But others clearly depict unexplained white blobs which many claim are either Abby or other forms of non-worldly energy.

Rama Patel said she has never had any close encounters with any kind of spirit in the hotel, but admitted that there have been incidents in which faucets and fans turn themselves off and on. "You see what you want to see," she said.

Mysteries such as this are common in Prescott. An anonymous contributor to the ghost chat room tells about seeing a woman holding a baby in the room she shared with a boyfriend in the Hassayampa Hotel, another of the city's older and highly regarded establishments.

Possibly even eerier is the ghost who lives in the Prescott Fine Arts Association theater just a few blocks south of the Hotel Vendome. The theater is housed in what used to be the Church of the Sacred Heart of Jesus, built between 1891 and 1895. A brick rectory next to the church was added in 1915. By the early 1960s the congregation had outgrown the church, so it moved to a new one. The old structure was converted to a combination gallery and theater in 1969, and the ghost began appearing shortly after that.

Local lore says it's the ghost of Father Edmund Clossen, an itinerant Catholic priest who worked among the Indian tribes and was affectionately known as Father Michael. The priest often stayed in the church and, so the story goes, once saved the life of a fellow priest by breaking down a door and rescuing him when a fire swept through the building. Father Clossen died under mysterious circumstances in 1902, and members of his Native American congregation brought his body to the church. He was originally buried under the altar but was later disinterred and reburied in a local cemetery.

But his ghost stayed on, according to some.

And now, when actors are getting into costume in the dressing rooms located in the old rectory, they say they hear the priest's ghost rattling the door on the second floor. One director claimed that he saw a shadow crossing in front of a painted moon on the back of a set. Then the director of the play *Blithe Spirit* told friends that one night after the audience had left, he and three actors were onstage making a postproduction check when three glasses rose from a bar then dropped to the floor and shattered.

As is the case with most ghost stories, some believe, others don't.

Rama Patel has adopted that philosophy. Although she talked freely about Abby and Noble, and any other ghosts that may be wandering around the hotel, she doesn't use them as marketing agents. The Vendome's brochures tout Prescott's ideal weather, the national forests filled with tall pines, nearby antiques shops, hiking trails, and fishing spots, but make only a brief reference to the two nonpaying guests: "Legendary, and full of history, the hotel is said to have had many owners since 1917, one so memorable, her friendly spirit is said to remain . . . in Room 16 . . . with her cat."

The scrapbooks grow along with the legend, Patel added. "We try to keep the scrapbooks credible with firsthand information, and we welcome those who believe and those who don't. It's not dissimilar to religion."

Then she concluded, "Abby is a good story, filled with an air of mystery and romance. So if there are ghosts here, I don't mind people calling them Abby and Noble."

CECIL CRESWELL:
ARIZONA'S LADY RUSTLER

A morning storm blew into the high desert, a blustery arrival that would rearrange the sands of northeastern Arizona then move on. But after the winds calmed, the land would still be much the same as before. Nothing much changes up here on the high desert.

Cecil Creswell got out of the creaking bed, fixed a meager breakfast, and went about the tasks associated with staying alive in a foreboding environment. There'd be chores, just like on all the other days. Livestock to be fed, fences to be fixed. And, probably, trespassers to order off the land. They were the worst part of living alone up here where only red sandstone monoliths interrupted the storms that scoured the landscape. The rifle was usually an effective persuader, but it was only a temporary solution. They would be back. Maybe not today. Tomorrow, however. Or the next day. Or some day soon. For sure.

But it would all end on this day.

The wind still howls across the barren land just east of Winslow where Cecil Creswell once tried to scrape out a living. It can be an inhospitable place, even under the best of conditions. And Cecil Creswell's conditions were never the best.

Cecil Creswell became a cowgirl and a rustler after a career as a Harvey Girl.

Despite the name, Cecil was a woman, and her life was a paradox. She ran away from home at an early age and became a socialite, then a cattle rustler. She had an open dislike for men but married at least three times, perhaps four. She was a crack shot with a rifle and frequently shot at people who crossed her, but the only person she ever hit was herself.

She fought the land, the elements, the neighbors, and the law in a lifetime cut short by despair and a bullet. Today, those who knew her and those who know about her say she was a kind person, a strange person, a loner, and a witch. But most of all, she is remembered as a lady cattle rustler, an occupation that gained her both notoriety and sympathy: the notoriety because female cattle rustlers were rare; sympathy because she wasn't in it for the money.

She wasn't always a rustler, of course. Cattle rustling isn't one of those career choices people select while in high school or college. She sort of drifted into the profession late in life, when times went from tough to really bad. Once she had been a sweet little girl from South Dakota who waited tables and smiled graciously at the customers in a posh hotel. But just like the plot of countless movies, fate began smacking her around until a trip down the criminal path became one of her few options.

Nobody knows how she came by the name Cecil. She was born Olive Dove Van Zoast in either 1892 or 1901, depending on her personal recollection or the courthouse statistics. She spent her formative years on the family farm near Olivet, a farming community just north of Yankton in the southeastern corner of South Dakota. The details of her early life are sketchy, but according to historians, she ran away from home at age fourteen and arrived in Winslow, Arizona, to work as a Harvey Girl in 1918.

The Harvey Girls were essentially waitresses, but they achieved national attention and acclaim because they were kind, courteous, well trained, and, most important, they often became lifetime companions for the lonely ranchers and cowboys who were trying to tame the land. In Winslow they donned their black-and-white uniforms and served the diners at La Posada, a Harvey House designed by Mary Jane Colter, the lodging chain's premiere architect. The Harvey Houses once stretched across the entire Southwest to serve the clientele of the Santa Fe Railway; by the year 2000 most of the buildings had been razed or converted to other uses. La Posada underwent extensive renovation in the late 1990s, and is the only Harvey House still in use as a hotel in Arizona.

Like many of her peers, Cecil found romance during her time as a Harvey Girl. There are conflicting stories about her love life, however. Some records say she was married once before her arrival out West. Others say her first husband was a railroad policeman from Winslow. That marriage didn't last because he was convicted of bigamy and sent to prison. Then she met and married George Creswell, a Bureau of Indian Affairs livestock inspector. The couple moved into his home in Tuba City on the Navajo Reservation, and the times were good.

Creswell provided her with a lifestyle that was comfortable, even a little above average for the times. And Olive Dove Creswell responded by becoming somewhat of a socialite who made friends easily and appeared regularly at the town dances. She was pretty and easy to like, a five-foot-four-inch, 120-pound bundle of energy with uncommon athletic skills and a great love of the outdoors.

But that phase of her life ended when George Creswell died in 1924. The Great Depression was on the horizon, and a single woman over thirty didn't have many career opportunities except remain a widow, get remarried, open up a boardinghouse, take in laundry, or seek menial tasks that barely paid a living wage. Olive Dove Creswell had one other option, however. Her husband's estate included a 160-acre homestead near Winslow. There was nothing there except bare ground dotted with hardy weeds that could withstand the harshness of the area. But she moved onto the property and began converting the land into a home.

The times were getting tougher. The Great Depression was no longer a figure looming on the horizon. It stomped across the country, draining pocketbooks and wallets, life savings and investments, and hitting the smaller communities with particular severity. The Creswell homestead, barren and arid even without the brutality of the Depression, became Cecil's temporary refuge. History indicates she had a couple of common-law arrangements after that, but they didn't work out. Charles Miller, a former Winslow resident who knew her when he was a child, said she once showed his mother a large scar on her breastbone. She said it was the result of a knife wound she suffered during one of her relationships.

But the loneliness and lack of finances eventually became so great that she married again, this time pairing up with Moon Mullens, a cattleman. Fate, however, wasn't done stirring up her personal tempest. Mullens was struck by lightning and killed in New Mexico in the early 1940s. It was about that time that Olive Dove

Creswell Mullens, apparently fed up with the hand dealt her as a woman, underwent a drastic personality change. She began using the name Cecil and started dressing like a man, wearing blue jeans, work shirts, and a big floppy cowboy hat. She devoted her energy to converting her homestead into a home, became a sharpshooter, and learned to ride a horse as well as any of her male contemporaries.

Although small, she was rugged. She toiled as a hired hand on area ranches to stay alive and was, according to those who knew her, about as good at riding, roping, and wrangling as any man. She also worked on her own place. With no help from anyone, she built a house, a chicken coop, a stone fence, and a mesquite fence and dug out a large catchment basin to hold water for her livestock.

Then she started borrowing livestock from other ranchers.

It is at this point in her life where history, morality, the code of the Old West, and public opinion take separate paths. There seems to be little doubt that Cecil was appropriating other people's livestock. But opinion is still divided on whether she did it as a matter of survival or because she was just plain ornery.

And although she turned into a recluse after the death of her last husband, she also became a public figure because of her brushes with the law and the neighbors.

One of the first recorded incidents occurred on June 6, 1949, when she was arrested and placed under peace bond for shooting at Sam Duran, an area rancher. In July 1952 she was fined three hundred dollars after being charged with fence cutting and trespassing. About a month later, she was accused of shooting a bull belonging to another neighbor, John Thompson. The charge was cruelty to animals; the fine was $150 and a suspended jail sentence.

Cecil and Thompson had a particularly bad relationship. Her property was next to his, and they had a long-standing feud over the boundary. According to a brief biography written by James E. Brisendine, a former sheriff's deputy, "Cecil hated John and he felt the same about her. They had a property line dispute years before and neither had ever forgotten it. One day, John was riding his horse a little too close to her fence. She took her .30.30 rifle and shot the horn off his saddle while he was in it. This almost frightened him to death. Old John went straight to the Superior Court judge and filed a complaint. The judge issued a warrant for Cecil's arrest."

About the only other times she appeared in Winslow were on rare occasions when she'd ride into town on a big black stallion named Pig that she had trapped and broken by herself. Her visits were brief. She'd trade beef from her ill-gotten herd for provisions with the local merchants. But sometimes she'd take the illegality of it all to another level. If she didn't have any cattle available for slaughter, she'd shoot a burro, butcher it, and pawn it off as beef.

And yet it wasn't the rustling that upset the townspeople so much. It was all that shooting. Bullets whizzed by the heads of cowboys, ranchers, hunters, and anyone else that came within shooting distance of her place. In one of the last interviews he gave before his death, Thompson told freelance writer Bob Thomas that she shot at him quite often.

Thompson, who died in 1997, told Thomas about a specific encounter with the woman that really got him rattled. "Once, when I was riding back, she was hiding in the bush and she called out to me, 'Hey, John.' I just froze," he told the writer. "I knew who it was.

I just kept on riding like I didn't hear her. Then she started firing and those big old bullets went past so close I could have reached out and caught them."

Dale Hancock is now a contractor in Winslow, but as a youth he worked on Thompson's ranch and vividly remembers being one of Cecil's targets. He was part of a fence-building crew when the lead started flying. "We saw her driving a small herd of Thompson's cattle toward her ranch, and when she saw us she grabbed her gun and started shooting. She kept us pinned down all day. Every time we started to move, she'd take a shot at us until it got too dark to see."

Hancock said he still doesn't think she meant to hit anyone, just scare them. "She made sure we knew she was around," he said in the summer of 2003. "She could have shot any one of us any time she wanted to. And when you're 14 years old like we were, that's enough to scare you."

After that, Hancock said, Thompson told his employees to carry guns when they were on the range near Cecil's place. That didn't slow her down one bit. Hancock said she took potshots at them almost every day and then, after they'd left for the day, she would ride along the fence line and rip up all the posts so the work had to be repeated the next day.

Her cattle-rustling enterprise was almost a thing of legend in the community. She needed a bull, so she stole one. It originally belonged to a neighbor, and it was originally light brown in color. Once she got it back to her ranch, Cecil managed to throw the bull to the ground and changed its brand to her Rafter 3. Then she disguised it. She took a bottle of henna hair dye and covered the bull's entire hide, converting it from a light brown creature to a dark red one. The ruse apparently worked so well that the neighbor later said he rode past Cecil's ranch almost every day and never recognized his property.

She also had to haul water from a creek to keep the herd alive. The creek was a half-mile away and her catchment basin apparently wasn't working, so she stole a fishing boat that was tied up at the creek. She used a lariat and her big horse to haul it back to her place, where she converted it into a stock watering tank. The original owner told authorities he never knew what happened to his boat until after Cecil's death.

Although her herd acquisition tactics were both illegal and blatant, there was a noticeable reluctance to do anything about it. Most people felt she wasn't stealing enough cattle to make that big a difference, while others said she was only trying to survive in an environment that was exceptionally hostile to single women. Not only were lawmen hesitant about dealing with a woman, particularly a sharp-shooting woman, there are rumors to this day that at least one of them regularly dropped off boxes filled with food and clothing at her front door.

But it had to end, and the final chapter in Cecil Creswell's life had even more ironic twists.

Despite her reputation, and despite all her earlier court appearances, she had never been charged with cattle rustling. Then on March 4, 1954, after a lengthy investigation by the Livestock Sanitary Board, she was formally accused of illegally appropriating the cows and horses of others. But the idea of confronting a little old white-haired lady who could shoot the eyes out of a rabbit from three hundred feet away didn't set well with those in charge of making the arrest, so they didn't tell Cecil about it. Instead, they resorted to treachery by luring her into Winslow on an undetermined legal matter. While she was in town, lawmen hustled to her ranch and removed all her guns.

All except one.

The next day, March 5, 1954, Navajo County Sheriff Ben Pearson and Deputy Brisendine went to the ranch, armed with a felony warrant that charged Cecil with illegally branding a horse that belonged to a neighboring rancher. According to a lengthy account printed in the *Winslow Mail*, they found Cecil working on a fence near the one-hundred-by-two-hundred-foot corral she had built using mesquite logs. "When told she would have to go into town with them," the newspaper account said, "she asked for permission to change clothes. This was granted and the officers were asked to come into the house and look at some of her paintings."

In his narrative Brisendine said the paintings looked as though a professional had done them. Her subjects were the surrounding landscape, wildlife, and desert scenes. He said the inside of her home was very feminine, not at all reflecting the lifestyle of its owner. With one exception. She had burned her Rafter 3 brand into all her furniture.

While the two lawmen and Cecil were in the house, Arden McFadden, the chief livestock inspector for the sanitary board, arrived at the ranch, accompanied by inspectors C. B. Griffin and Harvey Randal, and ranchers Rance Spurlock and Oscar Reid. They asked for permission to look around her spread for strays, and

Cecil gave her approval. "I have raised all this stuff from babies so I have nothing to hide," she said.

Reid and Spurlock unloaded their horses and began the search for new brands. On their first sweep, they found eight calves all wearing new Bar 3 Bar brands, another of Cecil's markings. Reid said they were all from his herd. Cecil denied it. She said they were born on her ranch and rebranded only recently because she'd heard there were cattle rustlers operating in the area. McFadden didn't buy the story. He ordered the calves clipped and checked for previous brands. They found Reid's original Four Dart brand.

Before long, they found twenty-one stolen cattle and one stolen horse, plus the remains of five butchered cows. Faced with such overwhelming evidence, Cecil remained calm and responded only that "it certainly was a Four Dart brand." Then she asked the deputy for a favor before being taken into Winslow.

The deputy later wrote, "I was leaning against the fence when she came over and asked, 'Jim, would it be okay if I walked up to the house to use the bathroom?' There was no way I could deny her the right to use her rest room, even though I was a little apprehensive about her going up to the house alone."

Seconds later, he realized his mistake. There was no bathroom in the house. In fact, there wasn't even an outhouse on the property. He said they should have brought a matron with them to deal with such a situation. But they didn't.

Right on the heels of that mistake, the lawmen realized that they might not have confiscated all her guns. Maybe they'd missed one. Coupled with Cecil's ability with a rifle, their close proximity to the house made them all prime targets. Their worst fears seemed to be coming true when the men heard a rifle shot. They scrambled for cover, aware that they'd been duped.

For a few minutes, they huddled behind whatever cover they could find. Then Pearson and Brisendine made their way to the front door and called for her to come out. Cecil had locked the door behind her, so the sheriff decided they should kick it down. Understandably, Brisendine was a reluctant partner to the plan. "I was not eager to do this," he wrote, "because we could be looking at the bad end of her .30.30 rifle."

But it didn't happen. In Brisendine's words, "We found the most heartbreaking thing that one could imagine. Cecil had put the barrel of the gun into her mouth and pulled the trigger. That was the single shot we had heard at the corral." So instead of facing death themselves, the lawmen found the body of an elderly woman who had lost her battle to survive. She had saved all her worn blue jeans, wrapped them with barbed wire, and stashed them under her bed. The rifle had been hidden in a pair of jeans.

But the bullet didn't quite end the drama that had been playing out for more than two decades. In her will Cecil left the ranch to an attorney who had befriended her. After a lengthy search, Brisendine found her sister in Utah, but the sister claimed the two had been estranged since the 1930s and were never close. Despite that, she made a brief visit to Winslow after the lawyer said he felt the property belonged to her. She accepted the deed and then, in one last twist of fate, sold it to John Thompson.

JAMES ADDISON REAVIS: THE MAN WHO CONNED ARIZONA

James Addison Reavis emerged from his prison cell on an April day in 1898. After two years behind bars, he was a free man. He was also penniless and friendless. His former associates had bailed out, his wife and children had left him, his empire had crumbled, and he had little hope for a future of any kind. But this was a man who had never let adversity stand in his way. He had built a fortune once; he could do it again. He'd be back on top.

But the old magic was gone now. He'd fail this time, and his life would end pretty much like it began—in poverty. So today the abbreviated rags-to-riches-to-rags life story of James Addison Reavis can be summed up in three sentences:

Born poor.

Lived rich.

Died poor.

Reavis was a man of many skills. They included lying, cheating, stealing, manipulation, forgery, bravado, wit, charm, and patience. He was clever, brazen, thorough, and silver-tongued, and he applied these talents liberally, all for his own benefit. He was a con man, but such a good one that even today, more than a century later, he is still considered one of the best at his chosen profession.

Between 1883 and 1895, Reavis controlled an area in Arizona and New Mexico larger than New Jersey. During that time, he was hosted by royalty, held counsel with congressmen, and owned several mansions. He also received large sums of money from railroads, mines, ranchers, even a newspaper, and not one cent of it was legally earned.

Naturally, a man of such ability, wealth, and power would need a lofty title, so he gave himself one—the Baron of Arizona. But like most other things in Reavis's life, it was a sham. He was not a regal person; he was a thief and a swindler. Unlike most others who select those occupations, however, Reavis got away with his crimes for more than a decade, and how he did it is still somewhat of a mystery.

His story had humble beginnings. Or royal beginnings, depending upon which version—his or the truth—is under consideration.

According to historical fact, it all started in Missouri on May 10, 1843, when Fenton and Maria Reavis had a baby boy whom they named James Addison. Fenton was an itinerant laborer; Maria was half Spanish. Her heritage played a major role in the development of her son's character because she taught him to speak, read, and write in Spanish, a factor that would later prove invaluable. She also filled his head with fanciful stories in which she portrayed herself as the daughter of royalty, and she told her offspring that the same royal blood now coursed through his veins.

When the Civil War erupted, it was Maria who influenced young James to join the Confederate army because she considered the Northerners crude and vulgar charlatans who were out to steal the family's birthright, small though it was. Because of that, she insisted, the war would result in a glorious victory for the South and, perhaps, a return to the lifestyle she claimed to have had in her earlier years.

Although the war didn't go quite the way the Reavis family expected, it did launch James on a journey that would lead to wealth that surpassed even his mother's wildest imagination. Bored with army life, Reavis

James Addison Reavis was the self-styled Baron of Arizona.

SCOTTSDALE COMMUNITY COLLEGE PHOTO

took up forgery. Small things at first. Overnight passes so he could slip into town, then passes for extended furloughs, then requisition papers for supplies which he sold to the local citizenry. His handwriting was so exact and so closely resembled that of his superiors that he was never caught. Not while he was a member of the Confederate army, at least. But when things started going bad for the Southerners, Reavis deserted and joined the Union forces.

That move, smart at the time, also led to one of his few failures. The handwriting of his Union army superiors was harder to copy. His forgeries were detected, and he deserted for the second time in the same conflict and left the country.

After spending time in Brazil, he returned to Missouri and worked in St. Louis as a streetcar operator, then a real estate agent, an occupation that prepared him for the career path he would eventually choose. He forged an old deed on faded paper, used the fake document to sell off some land, and made so much money on the deal that he realized there was a real future in swindling.

The facts move on to 1871, when greed entered Reavis's life in the form of Dr. George Willing. Known primarily as an eccentric who sold snake-oil medicines and grain alcohol to Indians and gullible settlers, Willing related a story about a land grant in the Southwest and it appealed to Reavis, even though it was far-fetched to the point of being unbelievable. Willing said that in the early 1860s, he encountered a desperately poor old Mexican man named Miguel Peralta near Prescott, in the Arizona Territory. Willing said he felt sorry for the man, so he traded money and supplies for a pack of old deeds which, Peralta claimed, were Spanish land grants.

Reavis was skeptical but interested. Such grants were still being honored by the United States government under the Treaty of Guadalupe Hidalgo, as long as the deeds were issued before the United States annexed much of the Southwest in 1848. Willing insisted that they could own more than two thousand square miles of land if they could find a way to validate the claims purported on the Peralta deeds.

Although suspicious, Reavis listened. He had heard about the land grants and also understood how easy it was to forge documents pertaining to them, and he saw an opportunity that he could convert into wealth. It might not be legal, but he had frequently extended his talents beyond the law, so that aspect of the venture was of little concern. The pair worked for almost two years trying to figure out how to make the deeds pay off, but gained little ground. Then a financial disaster in 1873 put an end to Reavis's real estate operation. He left St. Louis and decided to concentrate on the Peralta papers.

Reavis and Willing hatched an intricate scheme that involved buying the mineral rights to the claim, followed by secret meetings, extended travels, and appearances before federal officials. They were to meet in Prescott and file the claim, but when Reavis arrived, he discovered that Willing had died under mysterious circumstances that smacked of murder. But the coroner ruled it an overdose of whiskey and laudanum, and there were no charges filed.

Under ordinary circumstances, his partner's death would have forced Reavis to choose a different method of getting rich. But he was determined, and although he had never put much stock in Willing's story and the Peralta deeds, he realized that there would be other similar situations. So he returned to San Francisco, got a job as a newspaper reporter, and was sent to pacify Collis P. Huntington, a railroad tycoon who had been slammed by the paper. Instead, he told Huntington and his associates about the Peralta papers. He said that if the claim was approved, he would be able to help the railroad gain right-of-way privileges. But he needed money to study the claim. Not quite sure, but fearful that there might be some truth in his story and that he might take his offer to a rival rail line, the owners agreed to a two thousand dollar advance with a promise of royalties if things went as Reavis outlined them.

It was a start. Not much of one, but the plan was formulating in Reavis's cunning mind.

The railroad formally sent him to Arizona in 1880. Once there, he began researching Spanish land grants, how they were being handled in the territory, and, probably, people who might be swayed or paid to see things his way. Then, in a brilliant move that was to foreshadow the many that followed, he went to Prescott and conned Willing's family out of the deeds that had been left untouched since the doctor's demise. It was not an impressive collection. The writing on the documents was faded and barely legible, the witnesses to the exchange between Willing and Miguel Peralta were two itinerants, and the agreement was signed three years before Willing arrived in the territory. But Reavis saw them as a gold mine. If he could manipulate railroad tycoons into giving him money for rights to an unseen land grant, a more believable claim would be worth millions. And he had the tools and the skills to make it happen.

At this point in the story, the timetable shifts from the late 1800s to the early 1700s, and from actual fact to a masterful and well-written piece of fiction.

Reavis was careful and he was meticulous. Soon after acquiring the Willing papers, he traveled to Mexico, where he spent weeks examining documents in the state archives in Mexico City and Guadalajara. He pored over old land grants, royal proclamations, deeds, birth and death reports, and maps. He studied them over and over, noting the types of paper and ink used, the language, titles, and ranks, all the details that gave them authenticity.

He removed documents, forged copies, and returned the originals so nobody would become suspicious. He experimented with papers, inks, wax seals, and other elements involved in eighteenth-century transactions.

Then he created the Peralta family. And fiction appeared to become fact.

According to the phony Reavis version of history, the principal characters were high-born Spaniards who accumulated great wealth in the 1600s. His principal character was don Miguel Nemecio Silva de Peralta y de las Cordoba, born in 1708 into a family favored by royalty in both Spain and France. Don Miguel served in the military for several years then was given a title and sent to Mexico, where he looked after the king's interests. Because he handled his appointed duties so well, he was elevated to the rank of captain general and granted a large piece of land. Reavis also awarded his fictitious scion the title of "Baron of the Colorados."

Reavis was thorough. His forged papers tracked don Miguel and the Peralta grant for years, giving the fake aristocrat full title to the land in 1772. He visited his acreage only once, in 1778, when he established Arizonac, a small garrison near the ancient Indian ruin known as Casa Grande. According to Reavis, don Miguel then married at age sixty, sired a son at age seventy-three, and drew up a will that left everything to his family as "heirs to the Barony of Arizonac."

When the elder don Miguel died at age 116, his son inherited the estate and married a noblewoman from Guadalajara. They had a daughter whom they named Sofia, but they never moved to Arizonac because of the Civil War and the Indian uprisings. When economic pressure and revolution forced the collapse of his empire, don Miguel was left an impoverished old man, the same old man who traded a collection of old deeds to Dr. Willing.

One of those deeds was the Peralta grant.

At least, that's the way Reavis wrote it and that was the story he'd stick to.

Now he was ready to make his move. He arrived in Tucson on a hot September day in 1882, loaded with dozens of fake documents, some altered, some forged. His claims to a large chunk of land were met with incredulity, sneers, and doubt. But some also wondered if they might be real. This fear grew into a rumor, and the rumor spread across the territory. A short time later, landowners, sharecroppers, miners, railroad barons, and settlers were all expressing major concerns about their holdings.

The Surveyor General's office in Tucson was swamped with land grant claims, so Reavis left with his phony papers and traveled to San Francisco, where he began implementing another phase of his scheme. He befriended newspaper mogul George Hearst, who gave Reavis space in his *San Francisco Examiner* to publish non-bylined articles that hyped the Peralta grant. This was, in effect, valuable advertising for Reavis and his attempts to acquire investors for his land grab.

He returned to Tucson in less than a year, accompanied by Cyril Barratt, a disbarred lawyer, and Pedro Cuervo, who acted as a bodyguard and enforcer. They hauled several large containers of fake documents to the Surveyor General's office and demanded that Joseph Robbins, the man in charge, examine them and pass judgment about their worth. The more he examined, the more worried Robbins got. It appeared that Reavis might be legitimate.

Even worse, the claims had grown from the original 2,000 square miles that Willing had envisioned to an area that measured 75 miles by 250 miles. This was an 18,750-square-mile piece of land that included mountains, valleys, deserts, forests, mines, farms, ranches, the burgeoning city of Phoenix, and all the smaller towns that were springing up around it. It stretched from Phoenix to Silver City, New Mexico, and was larger than New Jersey and Delaware combined. If this claim was approved, Reavis would be one of the wealthiest men in the United States. Rather than make a quick decision on such a complicated situation, Robbins said he couldn't make a determination until he filed a report with the federal government, which was responsible for the final decision.

Emboldened that he had gotten this far with little difficulty, Reavis dipped into the investor money from San Francisco to build Arizola, a ten-room mansion erected on the site of some ruined foundations which he claimed were the original Peralta garrison. It was a fine home, quite suitable for one so powerful as the man who now called himself Baron de Arizonac Reavis. Now comfortable with his surroundings and confident that his claims would be upheld, Reavis unleashed his next maneuver—the shakedown.

Since all those farms, ranches, mines, and railroads were on his property, they owed him. And now it was time to pay up. He went after Col. James Barney first. Barney was president of the Silver King Mining Company and he buckled easily. Rather than lose an enterprise that was producing more than six million dollars a year, Barney coughed up twenty-five thousand dollars in blackmail money. Reavis gloated. Word would soon spread about this triumph. He would be unstoppable.

He next hired an army of mercenaries and gunslingers to post notices across the entire claim, ordering those on "his property" to either pay up or move out. Those who paid were allowed to stay, once they signed quit claims to their holdings in exchange for deeds of tenure and, of course, monthly rent. Those who resisted were initially threatened with six-guns and brute force. If they still held out, they were beaten, their livestock was stolen, and their farms burned. Reavis, naturally, denied any connection to such violence, and no one was ever able to prove that the thugs were acting under his orders.

Eventually those tactics backfired. His intimidated subjects rose up in protest, and the territorial newspapers started an angry media blitz against Reavis. They accused him of strong-arming his terrified tenants, and printed stories that his claims were being viewed with great suspicion by the Surveyor General. But the backfire had a backfire of its own when the *Phoenix Herald* revealed that Homer McNeil, editor of the *Phoenix Gazette* and a big property owner in Phoenix, had made a deal with Reavis to protect his own holdings. When that word got out, *Gazette* advertising fell off so badly that McNeil was forced to apologize and publicly cancel the transaction. He then exonerated himself by returning to the attack on Reavis.

Tom Weedin, publisher of the *Florence Enterprise*, a name-names and take-no-prisoners frontier weekly in Casa Grande, also climbed aboard the anti-Reavis bandwagon with great enthusiasm. He accused Reavis of extortion and brutality, and was so relentless that Reavis himself came to his office and offered Weedin a bribe to lay off. When the publisher refused, his family was threatened and his office was wrecked. Reavis denied any connection, but the incident brought renewed and more vigorous attacks by the frontier press.

Those efforts were finally recognized. In 1884 territorial Attorney General Clark Churchill filed suit against Reavis in an effort to further explore the land grant claim. Reavis was up to the challenge. During the court hearing, he produced letters and documents signed by railroad and mine owners that they had voluntarily complied with his requests and even invested money into his proposals. The case dragged on for a year before Churchill gave up and Reavis was allowed to continue. There were rumors that the federal government was willing to pay Reavis millions of dollars to relinquish his claim, but the offer was rescinded when a new administration took over. The victory in court made Reavis even bolder. He contacted Senator Roscoe Conkling of New York and asked him to help get the federal government's nose out of his business.

Then things started going bad. The Democrats won the 1884 election, President Grover Cleveland appointed Royal Johnson as the new surveyor general for the territory, and Johnson released a lengthy study that branded the Peralta land grant a fake. The word spread. Reavis was done for. His scheme collapsed, and he fled to California.

This would probably have been the end of the story if it had involved an ordinary man, even an ordinary con man. But James Addison Reavis was by no means ordinary. His days as a wealthy land baron were far from over.

While lying low in California, he turned once more to forgery and imagination, those talents that had served him so well before. Figuring that the best way to get his land back was to become legally tied to it, he invented doña Sofia Loreta Micaela de Maso y de Peralta, an heiress. In this intricately woven tale of deception, she married a shiftless Angeleno, who wasted the family fortune and impregnated her. Doña Sofia gave birth to twins, a boy and a girl. The mother and son died shortly after childbirth, the husband fled to Spain, and the orphaned girl was raised by John Treadway, a rancher in Mendocino County. While on a train trip when she was fifteen, the girl met a reporter named James Reavis, who said she looked a lot like doña Sofia, the last known Peralta heir. He started a friendship and, in his own words, was amazed when he found out that she actually was doña Sofia's daughter and therefore heir to the family fortune. According to this brilliant piece of fiction, Reavis was so smitten with the girl that he married her in 1882.

Now back to reality.

Reavis actually did meet Sofia Treadway on a train and, in his imagination, fancied that she looked like she could be an heiress. He befriended her and began relating his complex stories about the Peralta legend until he had her convinced that she was indeed an actual heiress. He gave her a new name—doña Carmelita Sofia Micaela de Peralta—and launched her on a fairy tale ride that would eventually take her to the royal houses of Europe. Again Reavis was clever and patient. He sent his protégée to a convent in San Luis Rey, where the sisters provided her with an education and, more importantly, the social graces that Reavis needed for his scheme. While she was in school, Reavis went to a church in San Bernardino and duped a priest into giving him access to parish birth records. Once he got hold of the register, he erased two spaces and inserted the names of the Peralta twins. Unfortunately for Reavis, the church kept a second set of birth records that he didn't know about. That would cost him later.

Also during this time, Reavis returned to Phoenix and rode out into a mountain range southwest of the city, searching for a big rock. When he found a suitable one, he etched some script and symbols into its face. They referred to the Peralta family and Spanish royalty. He would claim that this was the monument that marked the corner of his fictitious land grant.

When his fake doña graduated from finishing school, Reavis married her and became the Baron de Peralta. He took his bride to San Francisco, where he got financial backing to form a development company then floated a series of public shares which only he knew were worthless. Next he took his entourage to New York, where he renewed his acquaintance with Senator Conkling and used that influence, along with his well-honed powers of persuasion, to raise more capital for more scams.

Then it was off to Spain. Due to his ill-gotten wealth and his marriage to the title he had created, the swindler and his phony heiress were treated like royalty. They used this fake nobility to gain entrance into the courts and, more importantly, access into national archives in Madrid and Seville. He forged more documents by night and planted them in the archives by day. He also visited flea markets where he bought paintings of long-deceased unknowns. He passed these off as portraits of various members of the Peralta family to his new Spanish acquaintances and his new wife, who was not about to ask the questions that might terminate her time in this dream-come-true scenario.

They also went to England, where they were received by Queen Victoria. They even represented the Barony of Arizonac at her Golden Jubilee celebration, attended by most of the world's legitimate monarchy and royalty. But then came trouble at home. Dr. Willing's father was in court, claiming that he was the legitimate owner of the fake land grant that had started it all. Reavis hustled home, but the case, like almost everything else in the saga, was worthless.

The incident had an unexpected aftereffect, however—it renewed the hostility toward Reavis and his wealth. Reavis was typically undaunted. He forged ahead, expanded his development schemes, and formed the Casa Grande Corporation, which he claimed was worth five hundred million dollars. Investors snapped up his stock; Reavis made millions. He also retained Robert G. Ingersoll, a well-known reformist lawyer, to oversee his territorial operations while Senator Conkling took care of things in Washington.

All those safeguards weren't enough, however. The foundations of the Reavis empire were beginning to crumble.

He had been run out of the state once and now he was back, an even bigger braggart. He was perhaps the richest man in the territory; he was undoubtedly the most despised. When the word spread that he had resubmitted his claim to Surveyor General John Hise, the reaction was explosive. Suspicion and doubt turned to fear and hatred. In an editorial, the *Tucson Citizen* proclaimed that the solution to the Reavis situation was "a tall tree and a long rope." Wisely, Reavis didn't stick around during the furor. He traveled across the United States and Mexico, lauding his developments and soliciting investments. But back home, the end was getting closer.

Royal Johnson, who had labeled Reavis's claim a fraud years earlier, was reappointed as surveyor general and immediately sent a six-year study he had written about the Peralta grant to Washington. In his report, Johnson called the grant "fraudulent," "absolutely worthless," and "utter fiction." He noted discrepancies in the fake documents, and pointed out misspellings and bad grammar that were inconsistent with the wording that would have been used by the royal clerks. Experts examined the papers and found even more problems—eighteenth-century text written with nineteenth-century steel pens, typefaces from the wrong century, plus signs of erasures, write-overs, paste-ups, and other alterations. The evidence against Reavis was conclusive and damning, almost certain to hold up in any court.

In the face of all that, Reavis reacted in typical Reavis fashion—he sued the federal government for eleven million dollars, claiming that the allegations against him had ruined his development plans and cost him big bucks. In 1891 he took his suit to the Court of Private Land Claims in Santa Fe, a move that further hastened his undoing. The federal government assigned the talented attorney Matthew Reynolds as a special investigator. He compiled a mountain of incriminating evidence against the swindler and waited for the hearing.

Again Reavis was prepared. He hired witnesses to perjure themselves, restored his Arizola mansion, moved back in, and attracted a group of followers willing to support him in court. But the feds were even more determined. Agents sent to Spain discovered that he had been caught trying to steal documents. An investigator in San Bernardino uncovered the second set of birth records that had escaped Reavis's attention. His alleged witnesses confessed under federal grilling. Realizing that the end was near, most of Reavis's friends and all his financial supporters abandoned this sinking ship. When the case came to court, the former millionaire couldn't afford to hire an attorney and had to defend himself.

Reavis didn't even show up for the first three days of the hearing. During his absence, Reynolds built a devastating case against him that included allegations that he was a failed forger, a thief, and a fugitive from Spanish justice. Reavis finally showed up and tried to get the case dismissed on the grounds that it was irrelevant. His request was denied. In his own defense, he presented a rambling speech, sprinkled with name-dropping and flowery language, but it was in vain. On June 28, 1895, the court ruled that the Peralta land grant was mere fiction and pure fraud.

Reavis walked out of the courthouse, still determined to launch another land development scheme, but he had taken only a few steps when a federal marshal arrested him and hauled him back to face charges of attempted fraud, a criminal offense. This time it was over for good. Reavis couldn't afford to make bail and spent a year in jail awaiting his trial. Almost a year after his civil trial ended, he was sentenced to two years in federal prison and given a five thousand dollar fine, which he couldn't pay. His wife, the former sham third Baroness of Arizona, divorced him on the grounds of nonsupport, took their two children, and moved to Denver, where she spent her final days selling her story to various publications.

His reign as king of the con men had lasted for a dozen years, from 1883 to 1895. Although broke and destitute, Reavis refused to let go of his grandiose plans. After his release from prison, he tried for years to find new investors for new land schemes, but nobody was listening. Toward the end of his life, he was a decrepit old man who wandered the streets of Phoenix and read old newspaper accounts of his exploits in the public library. He lived his final days on a poor farm in Downey, California, close to where he had once served as a school principal.

Reavis did have a few more moments in the spotlight, although some were posthumous. He allegedly wrote a "confession" that appeared in a San Francisco newspaper in 1899. In it he said, "Until the very moment of my downfall, I gave no thought to failure. But my sins found me out, and as in the twinkle of an eye I saw the millions which had seemed already in my grasp fade away and heard the courts doom me to a prison cell." In 1950 he was the subject of *The Baron of Arizona*, a movie starring Vincent Price as Reavis and Ellen Drew as his wife. He is also the subject of a book by the same name, written by E. H. Cookridge.

Today only a concrete historic marker near Casa Grande shows where Reavis built Arizola, a spread that was once larger than the current city.

APACHE LEAP:
LEGEND, MYTH, OR FACT?

A good legend or myth should contain at least portions of several key elements. They include:

Traces of basic fact, generous amounts of believable fiction, a touch of mystery, healthy doses of skepticism, and overt hints of intrigue, all interspersed with well-weathered folklore, theory-based supposition, and some speculation, both biased and nonjudgmental.

Equally important, there should be no written records to support or disprove the legend.

But most of all, it must be a subject that is debatable for years, decades, even centuries, after the alleged actual fact.

The Legend of Apache Leap qualifies on all counts.

The incident upon which it is based may have actually happened. Or maybe it's simply another old folk tale.

If it happened, it was before 1865. Or after 1871.

The US Army may have been involved. Or it could have been a nonmilitary operation.

As many as eighty Apache warriors were killed. Or perhaps it was only twenty-five.

Only this much is absolute fact:

Apache Leap is a real place. It is a reddish, craggy bluff that rises more than two thousand feet above an area still known as Queen Creek Valley but now more commonly referred to as the town of Superior, Arizona. The bluff is composed of sedimentary stone layers from the Paleozoic era, and time and the elements have carved the layers into contorted shapes that resemble spires and monoliths with sharp edges. Or if viewers squint their eyes, the cliffs look like giant forests in which all the trees are made of rock. Either way, it is both fascinating and foreboding.

It rises 4,833 feet above sea level at the north end of the Dripping Springs Mountains, about six miles east of Picket Post Mountain. Near the bottom of Apache Leap, rock hounds still find pieces of obsidian encased in perlite. All these factors play important roles in the many versions of the story.

And now, on to the legend.

Interspersed with some history.

It's not a pretty story because it goes back to a time when white men considered Indians less than human. Apache tribes had roamed freely across the area since about AD 1500. They were diverse groups, involved in hunting, gathering, and farming. The Pinal Apaches, fierce and warlike, held dominion over much of the Pinal Mountains all the way up to the Mogollon Rim farther north. The Coyoteros developed pastures and small farms called "rancherias." The Tonto Apaches claimed the hunting and planting grounds in the shelter of the Tonto Basin.

Although they never banded together as one tribe, all three were united in their enmity toward the settlers who began arriving in the mid-1800s. They repulsed the intruders as long as they could, but eventually the tide overwhelmed the natives and developments sprang up along the rivers that fed the fertile land. Foremost among them was Florence Settlement a farming community that had been named after a sister of Richard C. McCormack, the second governor of Arizona Territory. This was a matter of great concern to the Apaches because Florence butted up against the edge of their lands. As a result, they retaliated.

Because it was so isolated, Florence became a target of continuous raids by the Apaches, who stole or drove away livestock and killed many of the settlers who rode the lonely trails between farms. In an effort to counteract the attacks, the federal government created the Arizona Military District and appointed Gen. George Stoneham as its commander. Once he arrived at his new post, General Stoneham realized that the only way to deal with the Apache threat was to establish military posts in the very heart of their territory, a sprawling area that many called Apacheria or Apacheland. The first post was originally named Camp Infantry, then later called Camp Pinal. But in the spring of 1871, General Stoneham moved the outpost to the base of Tordillo Peak and renamed the peak Picket Post Mountain. The army soon discovered that the top of Picket Post was an ideal site for watching the movements of the enemy, in this case the Apaches in hiding on top of Big Picacho, a red bluff six miles away, and the formation known today as Apache Leap.

From their positions on top of Picket Post Mountain, the soldiers used sunlight and mirrors to send signals by heliograph to lookouts on other mountains, thus protecting miners, freighters, and settlers from the raiders, whom they referred to as "the hostiles."

The Apaches, on the other hand, took a different view—they were defenders trying to protect their homelands from the white aggressors. So the raids continued. General Stoneham was relieved of his command before he could implement his plans for a major offensive against the Indians. Disgusted, he resigned from the army. The agricultural developments grew larger; the raids became more frequent. Time after time, the exasperated troops chased the marauders back into their mountain strongholds, and time after time, the clever Apaches vanished into the crevices and canyons.

Although they could never figure out how the Apaches got up there, the soldiers suspected there was a large rancheria on top of Big Picacho. They had seen the campfires and smoke signals and, occasionally, had spotted a lone Indian lookout perched on the jagged cliffs. But the knowledge was of little use to the army; all their military attempts to launch a campaign against the settlement were futile, primarily because they couldn't figure out how to scale the treacherous bluffs.

Eventually, however, the situation was resolved.

At this point, fiction and fact, folklore and legend, and speculation and supposition all converge, then dissipate into a variety of stories. This is one:

The Tonto Apaches called all their warriors together on top of the bluff and, in an apparent show of force, lit campfires along the summit as a prelude to an attack, a move probably designed to intimidate the troops. It didn't work. The army had discovered the secret pathway to the top, so the soldiers were able to sneak up during the night. They surrounded the encampment and, when dawn broke, they jumped the camp, shooting indiscriminately. Some of the Apaches fought back, but most of them leaped over the brink to their deaths on the sharp rocks below.

Here's another version, this one written by C. S. Scott in a 1914 magazine article:

> The [Apaches] and soldiers could plainly see each other from mountaintop to mountaintop, beyond the possible range of any arms that either had. The Indians felt secure and the whites were merely carrying out a strategic plan.
>
> By means of the heliograph, the [soldiers at Picket Post] signaled to scouts of the mountain party, who were instructed to always keep the Picket Post party in view, apprising them of the whereabouts of the Indians. The mountain party then stealthily crept up on the farther side of the big mountain in the rear of the Apaches and, assaulting them by surprise, wrought fearful havoc with their initial volley and followed up their bloody work as fast as possible. [Scott interjected here that there were women and children among the Apaches.]
>
> The Indians were panic-stricken and retreated in the only direction possible, toward the hither side of the mountain, which is a perpendicular cliff. It is said that many who did not fall before the rain of bullets threw themselves off the cliff in the hope of escaping fatal injury. Those of recent times who have been sufficiently curious and energetic to scale its forbidding cliff report the finding of beads, bones, and arrowheads, grim proofs of the essential facts of an incident of history that is fast entering the twilight zone

between authentic detail and legendary recital.

Historians counter such accounts as improbable for a couple of reasons. First, there are no Apache versions of the story, either in oral or written histories. Second, there is no mention of such an incident anywhere in the military records of the period. This leads to the speculation that something similar may have actually occurred, but it involved only a few people. However, as the story grew and the years passed, more victims were added.

Or, as others believe, the episode might have happened in the 1860s, during a time when volunteers and vigilantes were dealing with "the Indian problem," which might account for the lack of military records. The Arizona Volunteers, in fact, are credited with being the cause of the legend in another version, this one based on a document on file at the Arizona Mining and Mineral Museum in Phoenix, linking the fable to a specific military action in the winter of 1871. The paper says that Capt. John Walker led the Pima Indian troops of Company B, First Arizona Volunteers, on the raid atop Big Picacho.

"Nearly 50 of the band of 75 Apaches were killed in the first volley of shots," according to that rendition. "The remainder of the tribe retreated to the cliff's edge and chose death by leaping over the edge rather than die at the hands of the attackers."

There's a flaw in that story, however. The First Arizona Volunteers was a militia unit composed of Mexicans and Native Americans, formed to track down Apaches in 1865 when most regular solders were away fighting in the Civil War. The unpaid volunteers allegedly killed more than one hundred people before disbanding in 1866, five years before they allegedly staged the surprise attack on top of the mountain.

But that version is upheld by a similar version, this one written by James M. Barney and published in the October 1940 edition of *Arizona Highways*. Reprints of Barney's story are now handed out by the Superior Chamber of Commerce as the "official story of how Apache Leap got its name."

The text relates that the Apaches raided a ranch near Florence and drove away some cattle. The ranchers and farmers enlisted the aid of friendly Pima Indians, organized a vigilante posse, and patiently followed the trail of the raiders for several days. The Pimas were led by Capt. John Walker, a member of an Illinois tribe and Civil War veteran. He left the army and settled among the Pimas, learned their language, and became one of their chiefs and medicine men. When the Arizona Volunteers were formed, Walker raised Company B, composed entirely of Pimas, and was named their captain. Now called into duty, the company found the secret pathway leading to the Apache encampment.

According to this account, the Apaches had made a fatal mistake. Apparently feeling perfectly safe in their secret hiding place, they neglected to post lookouts. The oversight enabled the Pimas and settlers to sneak into the area under cover of night and surround the inhabitants on three sides. At daybreak, they attacked.

"Menaced on three sides by continuous gunfire," the story said, "the Apaches at first fired a few shots at their assailants, then—noting the helplessness of their situation—threw down their weapons and, with raised hands in token of surrender, advanced toward the attacking party. The latter, sensing their advantage and remembering the cruelties that these same Apaches had inflicted upon murdered comrades, refused to accept their surrender and continued to pour a murderous fire into them. Those found in the Indian rancheria included women and children, but in the excitement of battle, the attacking party paid little heed to the sex or age of their enemies."

When about two-thirds of the Apache inhabitants of the rancheria were killed by the hail of bullets, the rest retreated in the only direction left open to them—to the west, where the edge of the mountain broke off into sheer cliffs hundreds of feet high. "Without a moment's hesitation," the narration continues, "the fleeing Apaches threw themselves over the towering cliffs in the faint hope of escaping fatal injury. But the leap into space was too great, and all those who sought that avenue of escape were crushed and broken on the rocks below."

When the carnage was over, the story relates, the entire Apache band of seventy-five had been killed. There were no casualties among the attackers, and the decisive defeat broke the power of the Apaches in the region. The author concluded his narration with the observation that, from that day, Big Picacho has been known as Apache Leap, "a most appropriate name, perpetuating, as it does, a tragic incident in the early history of Arizona. For years after the bloody engagement, Apache skeletons could be seen wedged in the crevices of the cliffs over which they had leaped. . . . Those who have been sufficiently curious and energetic enough to scale the rough and broken slopes of the big mountain report finding bleaching bones and beads and arrowheads and other reminders of the conflict that took place."

Two other historians have given similar accounts. In his 1884 book, *History of Arizona Territory Showing Its Resources and Advantages with Illustrations*, Wallace W. Elliott discussed Apache warrior raids in the area near Florence. He noted that many settlers were killed and their homes burned until the Florentines armed themselves and followed the Apaches after one particular raid. Several days later, they found the trail leading to the hideout and retaliated.

In 1918 author and historian Thomas Edwin Farish repeated that version when he published his *History of Arizona*, Volume I. Both writers said fifty Apaches died in the onslaught and not a single warrior escaped. But at this point, both diverged from other accounts by writing that the group from Florence didn't harm any women and children but instead captured them and turned them over to General Stoneham and his US Cavalry stationed at Camp Pinal.

Many other stories have also dealt with the subject through the years. Most agree that the incident did occur, but they also include noticeable differences. In one written history of Superior, there's a line that reads: "The escarpment called the Apache Leap Mountain acquired its legendary name after a roving band of seventy-five Apache warriors rode their horses off the mountain to their deaths thousands of feet below in order to avoid capture by the US Army in a small skirmish atop the mountain . . . Arizona historians, however, say there is no historical basis for this story."

A 1998 motorcycle travel magazine article reported: "Legend has it—and it may very well be legend only and not fact—that the sheer red cliffs which loom over Superior, Arizona, are called

Obsidian, a highly valued stone, can be found in abundance at Apache Leap.

Apache Leap because, well, that is exactly what happened there way back when. As the story goes, in the 1870s, when the United States Cavalry was busily shoving the natives aside for the benefit of incoming settlers, a group of soldiers from nearby Camp Pinal managed to pin down a band of 75 Apache warriors who were camped up on the red bluff. Preferring death to surrender, the Indians turned to the west and rode their horses over the edge of the 500-foot cliff."

Another history of the town relates: "There is, however, still another, if not physical, reminder of the early presence of US Troops in the region [and] the origin of the Apache Leap legend can be traced to these troops. Although no official record exists of a skirmish between troops and Indians at what is now called Apache Leap, it is very likely that the legend has basis in fact."

As the story was told and retold over the decades, another chapter was added, and in it speculation became irrelevant, obsidian became an important element, and actual fact was replaced with poignant fantasy. Because this second part separates itself from all historical accounts, it has become the stuff of pure legend, unobstructed by certification of any kind.

But again, there is one small piece of truth involved: Obsidian is real.

It is a glasslike byproduct of volcanic eruptions, originally named "obsidianus" in Pliny's *Natural History* because of its resemblance to a stone found in Ethiopia by Obsius. It's hard, usually dark-colored or black, and is frequently used as a gemstone. The stones are translucent and often coated with a white, flaky material known as perlite, which has a variety of commercial uses, including one as a soil amendment. After a volcano has erupted and the debris it ejected has cooled, its obsidian flows can become fractured and hydrated over the millennia so the original glass is reduced from large sheets to small nuggets, varying from pea to baseball size and displaying a good clarity when held up to a bright light.

It was valued in Stone Age cultures because, like flint, it could be easily chipped and formed into sharp objects such as arrowheads and blades. Native Americans traded obsidian throughout North America, and it still has several practical uses. It is sometimes utilized in cardiac surgery because blades of well-crafted obsidian are sharper than high-quality steel scalpels. Lapidarists and rock hounds like obsidian because, depending on how it's cut, it presents different colorations that range from jet black to glistening gray.

But it is also a key element in the legend of Apache Leap. According to folklore, upon hearing of the massacre the next morning, the wives and mothers of the slain warriors gathered a short distance from the base of the cliff. When they found the broken bodies of their husbands and sons, their grief was immense. Filled with sorrow, they began mourning on the spot and the tears they shed fell to the white sand on the ground and were turned to stone.

And now, the stones are known as Apache tears.

It's a romantic and heart-rendering tale but, unlike the story behind the legend of Apache Leap, it has no factual support whatsoever. However, that has had very little effect on the continued telling and retelling of the story. Even today, there is a belief that although obsidian is common to many places across the world, only those found at the base of Apache Leap can be legitimately called Apache tears. And those who possess Apache tears will never have to cry again because the Apache women wept enough for all mankind.

Black obsidian is still considered a powerful meditation stone that supposedly dissolves suppressed negative patterns and then purifies them. And Apache tears can, according to some, balance the emotional nature and protect the stones' owners from being cheated in business dealings even while producing clear vision and increasing psychic powers.

But just like the legend itself, most of these claims have no basis in either science or fact.

PEARL HART: THE LAST STAGECOACH ROBBER

In the early morning hours of May 29, 1899, in the mining town of Globe in the Arizona Territory, Pearl Hart arose from her bed after a fitful night's sleep and got dressed. But she did not follow her usual procedure. She was going to hold up a stagecoach, and that would require a drastic departure from her normal routine. So on this day she tucked her hair into a cowboy hat, slipped her dainty legs into a pair of men's trousers, and did her best to look like someone other than Pearl Hart.

A legend was about to be born.

In hindsight, it becomes apparent that few, if any, of the misfortunes that befell Pearl Hart would have occurred if she had been more selective about her choice of male companions. Before she was thirty years old, she consorted with a professional gambler, jail escapee, stagecoach robber, sheriffs, deputies, scandal-seeking newspaper reporters, prison wardens and guards, jailhouse denizens, and several men who willingly parted with their wages to briefly enjoy her companionship.

Also in hindsight, all the bad things that happened to her happened because she loved her mother.

She spent most of her formative years trying to better herself, to become someone other than the daughter of a Canadian civil engineer. Eventually she did get to be famous, but in an infamous way. Now she is remembered primarily as the only lady stagecoach robber to ever appear on stage portraying herself.

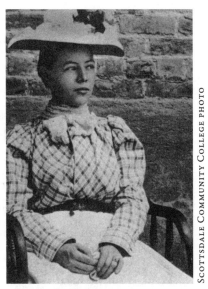

Pearl Hart was America's last stagecoach robber.

She was born Pearl Taylor in 1871, in Lindsay, Ontario. Her parents were middle class, but wealthy enough to send her to finishing school, where she was described as an excellent student although sometimes disrespectful of her elders. Bored with school and seeking a more exciting life, she made the first of many bad decisions when she eloped at age sixteen.

Her husband's last name was Hart. Historians disagree on his first name but have narrowed it down to Frederick, Brett, or William, with Frederick gaining the majority of the votes. He was a professional gambler and not very good at his trade. The couple spent their first years together doing odd jobs in restaurants, hotels, and saloons. Hart's successes at the gaming tables were small and infrequent. He also had a bad temper that worsened when he drank. As his failures at gambling increased, so did his drinking. Inevitably, that combination led to verbal abuse which led to beatings.

Fearing for her safety, Pearl took their young son and fled back to her family in Canada. The reunion was short-lived. Before the marital split, Pearl and her husband had gone to Chicago for the World's Columbian Exposition. He figured he could ply his gambling skills on the unsuspecting tourists. Apparently they weren't as gullible as he expected, and his grandiose plan to get rich vanished. So he took a job as a carnival barker, and Pearl had to go to work again. During that period, she became enamored of the Wild West shows being staged as part of the exposition, and became infatuated with one of the cowboys. According to accounts of that time period, the cowpoke gave Pearl the money she needed to escape from the beatings. When she had her son safely stashed with her parents, she succumbed to the lure of the West and moved to Trinidad, Colorado, then to Phoenix, in the Arizona Territory.

The romance of the Old West wasn't what she had expected, however, so once again Pearl was forced to compromise to survive. This meant more menial labor and, probably, clandestine meetings for money.

And unbeknownst to her at the time, all this was leading up to the incident of May 29, 1899.

But then, in one of her darkest hours, her life seemed to take a turn for the better. The abusive husband she had fled years earlier showed up in Phoenix. He had contacted her family to find where she'd moved, and now he came to her with the promise that he was a changed man who would never again lay a hand upon her, either in anger or in drunkenness. Pearl made another bad decision. She took him back. For a while it seemed like it might work. Hart gave up gambling as a livelihood and found work as a hotel manager;

Pearl worked as a cook and a maid, and the reunion produced a daughter.

There was not, however, a happy ending.

After about five years of togetherness, Hart announced that he was sick of being a husband and tired of being chained to a family. He told his young spouse that he wanted out, then joined the US Army with no apparent remorse about leaving a wife and child destitute on the streets of Phoenix. Alone again, Pearl got along as best as she was able, living pitifully on the meager wages she earned at domestic chores and, probably, prostitution. She also tried to kill herself on at least three occasions, but acquaintances stopped her every time.

Once again Pearl Hart was forced to call upon her family for help. She sent her daughter to Toledo, Ohio, where her parents had moved, then she migrated to the mining camps in the territory's Pinal Mountains.

And the episode that would make her famous drew closer.

Camp life was hard, but she found work as a cook for a mining company in Mammoth. The pay was minimal, and her situation got even worse when the letters from home began arriving. Each letter said her mother's health was deteriorating. The family needed money. Pearl had none to send.

At the same time, she befriended Joe Boot, a miner. He said they could earn more money if they moved to Globe. They entered into a loose partnership and tried to make it big by working a small mining claim. But theirs was not a success story. The riches never came. They started a hauling company to carry supplies to surrounding mines. The result was the same. And the letters from home kept coming, and each one described her mother's health as worsening. Pearl Hart was becoming more desperate. Then a telegram arrived; it said Pearl's mother was dying. Pearl had to come home to be at her bedside. Years later, she wrote, "That letter drove me crazy . . . I had no money. I could get no money. From what I know now, I believe I became temporarily insane."

May 29, 1899, was getting closer.

She told Boot about her troubles. He came up with a possible answer—they should rob a stagecoach. She was reluctant; he was forceful. It would be easy, he said. Nobody robbed stagecoaches anymore, he said, so the stage lines wouldn't be expecting a holdup. Also, he said, due to the infrequency of armed robberies, there wouldn't be a shotgun-toting guard on board to dissuade them. It was, he said, a perfect plan.

Pearl said she'd think about it. She did. Then she made another bad decision. She agreed.

May 29, 1899, had arrived.

Pearl Hart was about to become both famous and infamous.

Pearl and Boot left Globe on horseback long before the stage to Florence with its three passengers and driver pulled out. Pearl had cut her hair short and tucked what remained under a cowboy hat. Then she put on some of Boot's clothing, which didn't fit her very well because she was only five-foot-two and weighed around a hundred pounds while Boot was a five-foot-six 150-pounder. They rode their horses southwest of Globe to Cane Spring. The dirt road made a sharp turn, so the stage would have to slow down. And then they waited.

When the coach came around the curve, Arizona's first and only female stagecoach robber and her accomplice drew their pistols and screamed at the driver, "Elevate!" Taken by surprise, he threw his hands into the air. Boot kept his gun aimed at the driver while Pearl turned her pistol toward the passengers and ordered them out of the coach. When they complied, she searched each one and removed their money, about $425. Then, in a move that surprised everyone at the scene, she gave each passenger one dollar so they'd have enough to buy food when they reached Florence. As the robbers were leaving, Pearl Hart made another bad mistake when she grabbed the driver's six-gun. Then they rode off into the surrounding desert.

While the robbery went off without a hitch, nothing else went according to plan, if there ever was a plan. Being novices, the duo had neglected to figure out how they were going to get to Benson, where they hoped to catch a train that would take them miles away from the scene and eventually to Canada. With no maps or established routes to guide them, they got lost several times and left an easily followed trail through the desert underbrush. Meanwhile, the stage continued on to Florence, where the driver told Pinal County Sheriff W. E. Truman that he recognized the robbers. The sheriff formed a posse of armed horsemen and they left at once.

It took less than four days for the capture. Exhausted and soaked by a spring rain, Pearl and Boot made camp in a small cave. Boot started a fire. They removed their guns and some of their clothing to let them dry out, then fell asleep. This made it easy for the posse. They surrounded the pair, sneaked in and removed their guns, and woke them up with the news that they were under arrest. Boot gave up easily. Pearl didn't. She sprang up fighting, and snarled that she would have shot all of them if they hadn't taken her gun away. Sheriff Truman later told a reporter for the *Tucson Citizen*, "One wouldn't think that she is a very tiger for nerve and endurance. She looks feminine enough now, in the women's clothes I got for her, and one can see the touch of a tasteful woman's hand in the way she has brightened her cell. Yet, only a couple of days ago, I had a struggle with her for my life. She would have killed me in my tracks could she had got to her pistol."

The couple was jailed in Florence and charged with armed robbery. Not just any armed robbery, however: the first stagecoach robbery ever pulled off by a woman. And although nobody realized it at the time, it would also be the last stagecoach robbery in the United States. The inevitable media circus soon followed. The woman bandit was big news all across the nation. The highly competitive newspapers of the day sent reporters to Florence in the hope of producing sensational trial stories. *Cosmopolitan* magazine, still in its infancy, asked for an interview. The *New York Times* used stringers to cover the incident. Pulp magazines and dime novels, the most popular forms of reading material at the time, exploited the situation through a blend of fact, fiction, and fancy.

Sheriff Truman didn't like it. He said all the publicity was "extremely annoying," and therefore opted to send Pearl to the Pima County Jail in Tucson while keeping her partner in the Florence facility. This did not deter, or even slow up, the sensationalism being generated by the case. Once the basic facts had been discovered and distorted, the reporters began working on new angles. In time many of them converted Pearl Hart from sinner to saint, elevating her from holdup artist to a sympathetic figure who had good reasons for committing the crime. A few even depicted her as a women's libber, long before that term came into popular use. She was, according to one report, "a strident voice for women's emancipation." Many others picked up a quote she had allegedly used in the Florence jail, when she said that she would "never consent to be tried under a law she or her sex had no voice in making, or to which a woman had no power under the law to give her consent."

Her notoriety grew. Jail guards started hanging around her, some even asking for her autograph. They created what one account said was "an enthusiasm that was harmful to discipline." The newspaper reporters were her constant visitors, digging into both her past and her frame of mind, questioning her about the men in her life and how she felt about the danger of leading a life such as the one she had chosen.

A lot of that fuzzy good feeling toward her vanished a short time later. While incarcerated in Tucson, she became friends with an inmate trustee known as either Ed Hogan or Ed Sherwood, serving time for petty theft. This led to another error in judgment by Pearl Hart. Hogan (or Sherwood) became emotionally fond of the woman and, because he was allowed to roam the jail rather freely, helped her escape on October 12, 1899, by cutting a hole through the thin wall of her cell. They fled together and got as far as Deming, New Mexico, before local lawmen recognized them, arrested them, and returned them to Florence. There, although she still hadn't consented to be tried under what she considered an unfair law, Pearl was forced to face Judge Fletcher Doan and a jury.

Before her trial began, she made a flamboyant, though facetious, attempt at suicide. While a guard stood directly in front of her cell, she screamed that she no longer wanted to live and hurled some white powder into her mouth. The guard called a doctor who examined the woman, then told her to quit faking because, he said, "No one ever killed themselves by swallowing talcum powder."

Her fate now lay in the hands of the jury.

Speaking on her own behalf, the lady bandit played the sympathy card, telling the jurors about her dying mother and repeating her earlier statements about the laws being unfair to her gender. Apparently it worked. The jury met for less than an hour before returning a verdict of not guilty.

But if Pearl felt she had escaped the long arm of the law, it was only a momentary belief. Judge Doan wasn't about to let her off so easily. Furious, he read the riot act to the first jury, empanelled a new jury, then had her rearrested for stealing the stagecoach driver's six-shooter during the holdup. The new jury debated for less than fifteen minutes before finding her guilty. The *Tucson Citizen* reported that "the judge decided it would take five years of discipline in Yuma [Territorial Prison] to cure her of the practice of holding up a stage." Joe Boot received a thirty-year sentence on the original charge and was also sent to Yuma, where he became a trustee and was allowed to drive a freight wagon. One day he simply drove away from the prison and was never heard from again.

Once she got settled down in a prison cell specially prepared for her, Pearl went about her business of being a famous person. As the prison's most celebrated inmate, she was given a small side yard adjacent to her cell, and was allowed to grant interviews.

An ever-increasing number of legitimate journalists and fiction writers compiled prose about her love for cigars, her ability to cuss like a mule skinner, and how she strutted around her quarters behaving like a lady bandit should. She also agreed to pose with unloaded firearms, then went through a period when she acquired religion and began spreading the gospel. She gave fellow inmates long lectures on how to avoid the

SCOTTSDALE COMMUNITY COLLEGE PHOTO

The story of Pearl Hart inspired a number of writers and filmmakers.

ways of the sinner, warning them that crime only leads to places like Yuma Territorial Prison. Word of her evangelism and apparent rehabilitation spread outside the prison walls, and a group of Arizona citizens petitioned for her release. After serving eighteen months, her sentence was commuted and Pearl Hart was set free.

But there's more.

Many historians don't think it was her religious beliefs that got her out of jail early. In fact, it was something quite the opposite. According to their versions, Pearl was pregnant at the time. This had the earmarks of a major scandal because the only men she had any contact with during her incarceration were the prison guards, the warden, the chaplain, and, worst of all, Territorial Governor Alexander W. Brodie, the man who ordered her release. The stated reason was that the prison had no accommodations for women, but many winked at that explanation and spread the inevitable rumors. However, there is no record of her giving birth to a third child, so the rumor may have been an attempt to get out of prison early. If that was the case, it worked.

As a provision of her release, Pearl had to agree to leave Arizona Territory and never return. She promised and left the area in late 1902, headed for Kansas City. The *Yuma Sentinel* recorded her departure with this observation: "Quite a large number of people were at the depot to get a glimpse of Arizona's famous female ex-bandit and they were not disappointed for she was there, and if there is one thing more than another that Pearl is not shy on, it is a fondness for notoriety."

After arriving in Kansas City, she moved in with her mother and sister. The *Sentinel*'s report noted that the sister "has written a drama in which Pearl will assume the leading role. . . . The drama will embody Pearl's own experience as a stage robber, with all the blood and thunder accompaniments, and the famous Pearl will once again, with her trusty Winchester, hold up the driver of a western stage, line up the passengers and relieve them of their valuables."

The play, entitled *The Arizona Bandit*, got on the Orpheum circuit but did not do well. One critic noted that "Pearl Hart portrays herself with all the enthusiasm of a pile of rocks," a rather brave observation considering that the object of his scorn was armed with a Winchester. When the show closed, Pearl managed a cigar store in Kansas City, but her troubles weren't over. She was arrested, charged with receiving stolen canned goods and running a gang of pickpockets, and did more jail time.

The rest of her life is sketchy. Some sources say she served her time then moved to San Francisco, where she allegedly died in 1925. The more popular versions say she moved to New York, worked under an alias in Buffalo Bill's Wild West Show, then returned to Arizona and married Calvin Bywater, who operated a ranch near Globe. According to this theory, she lived a quiet and much more private life for her last fifty years before dying on December 30, 1955, at the age of eighty-five, and is buried in a cemetery in Claypool, halfway between Globe and Miami. Credibility for this story line came from Clara T. Woody, a newspaper writer who said she discovered that Pearl Bywater was actually Pearl Hart while Woody was working as a census taker in 1940. She said Mrs. Bywater's room was littered with cigar butts and that she was "sloppily dressed," but did not explain why she made the connection. Other accounts relate much of the same information, but say Pearl's grave site is in Hayden, not Claypool.

Another story says she eventually returned to Florence and visited the courthouse where she was tried and convicted. She observed that "the place hasn't changed much," and when asked about her identity, she replied, "Pearl Hart, lady bandit."

Under any circumstance, the life of Pearl Hart ended a long time ago. But the legend survives. She has been the subject of *The Legend of Pearl Hart*, a musical production that ran in New York in 2006; a play titled *Lady With a Gun* that was staged in Prescott in 2002; and the movie *Legend of Pearl Hart*, filmed in 2007 but never released. She has also been the subject of countless books, historical references, and never-ending speculation.

THE RED GHOST: FICTIONALIZED FACT OR FACTUAL FICTION?

Any story that purports to be the true story of the Red Ghost must include a cast of characters that includes Edward Beale, Hi Jolly, Mizoo Hastings, an unnamed woman, George Crosman, Jefferson Davis, Cyrus Hamblin, Henry Wayne, David Porter, and John Floyd.

The story must be spiced with allegations and hearsay, historical fact and frontier fantasy, the deserts of Arizona and sands of North Africa, military mismanagement and camel husbandry. Camels are paramount to any version because the Red Ghost, in truth and in folklore, was a camel. There are documented facts and hints of fiction to support all contentions, and each version plays a vital role in any narration involving the specter that roamed the Arizona deserts so long ago.

Archaeologists maintain that camels inhabited what is now Arizona and the rest of the North American continent millions of years ago, migrating across land masses to Africa and the Middle East even as they slowly died out here. But one species of camel persisted until a mere (by geological standards) fifteen thousand years ago. Their bones and other remnants are still being found along the California coast. However, they are of interest only to those who mine the elusive relic and hunt the rare fossil. It is the latter-day camels that spark the curiosity of the modern tellers of campfire tales, ghost hunters, and even the occasional liar.

First the alleged true story that brought the Red Ghost into prominence. Then the probable causes.

In the spring of 1883, two women were left alone with their children in a small adobe house on a sheep ranch along Eagle Creek in the southeastern corner of Arizona Territory. Being alone on the frontier was always an uncomfortable and dangerous situation, but the women were accustomed to it. Life in the harsh desert had hardened them. The men were gone frequently; this time it was to determine how many of their livestock had been slaughtered or driven off by a band of marauding Apache warriors, supposedly led by the fabled Geronimo. Although aware of the peril, one of the women left the house to replenish the water supply. The spring was only a few yards away from the house, but it was hidden by a stand of willow trees. Shortly after the woman disappeared into the thicket, the family dogs began howling so loud that the other woman ran to the window. As she stood there, she was frozen by the horror of the scenario that was taking place in front of her.

She heard screams and saw a huge beast that was, she recalled later, "red, enormous, and ridden by a devil." Too terrified to even think of going outside, she barricaded herself and the children inside the house and spent the remainder of the day on her knees, praying that the men would return soon. Night had fallen when they got back. She composed herself enough to relate the story; the men lit torches and went outside to investigate. When they reached the spring, they found the other woman's body trampled almost beyond recognition. The mud surrounding her corpse was filled with huge cloven-hoof prints, many times larger than that of a sheep and almost twice the size of an imprint made by a cow or horse. They also found strands of long red hair clinging to the willows.

The body was taken to nearby Solomonville, where a suspicious coroner held an inquest. He thought it had some earmarks of a murder. Maybe a family member had done it. Life on the frontier often produced family tensions that sometimes resulted in violence. But the horribly battered body and the oversize footprints led him to dismiss such thoughts. When he was finished with his inquiry, he ordered the jury to bring in a verdict of "death by some manner unknown." The *Mohave Miner*, a weekly newspaper in Kingman, reported the ruling but gave no further details.

The woman's bizarre death might have gone relatively unnoticed except for an incident that happened a few days later in the same area. Two prospectors panning for gold in Chase's Creek were unexpectedly awakened in the middle of the night when their tent came crashing down on them. They heard what they described as "a loud scream and the sound of pounding hoofs." What they saw was even more frightening—an animal much too large to be a horse, galloping off into the surrounding brush. The two gold seekers rushed into a nearby mining camp and told their story. Several other miners, probably in disbelief, followed them back to their claim. What they found made the hair on the back of their necks stand straight up. Along the creek bed, they discovered huge hoofprints that led up a small hill. The prints had obviously been made by a large animal, much larger than any of the domesticated stock used by the miners and ranchers. And they also found a few long red hairs clinging to the undergrowth. After comparing the two incidents, those involved came to a conclusion. The creature was a camel.

The legend of the Red Ghost was about to become a chapter in Arizona folklore.

The observation that a wild camel was causing so much damage was not surprising, considering the circumstances. Camel sightings were rare but not uncommon in the territory. In the mid-1850s the US Army launched what became known as the Great Camel Adventure, an experiment that failed miserably for both humans and camels.

The region's climate was fit for neither man nor beast, but they came anyway. First came the miners, then the settlers, all determined to extract riches from the arid desert. Their presence sparked conflicts with the natives already on the land, so military involvement soon followed. But the punishing climate and rugged terrain took their toll on the horses and mules that were traditionally used by the army as mounts and pack animals. Then someone suggested camels as alternatives. The idea was met with ridicule and opposition by most, but others thought it was sound. Among them was Lt. George Crosman, an army veteran of the Seminole campaigns in Florida. Crosman reasoned that "for strength in carrying burdens, for patient endurance of labor and privation of food, water and rest, and in some respects for speed also, the camel and dromedary are unrivaled among animals."

In addition, Crosman observed, camels could carry burdens up to four times heavier than a mule could, they could travel up to forty miles per day for extended periods, and could go without water for six to eight days. These factors would make them ideal for the Arizona desert, he argued. His logic was sound, but no one took Crosman seriously as he presented his case to both army and political figures. But his luck changed when he met and befriended Maj. Henry C. Wayne, an army quartermaster.

Wayne knew people in high places. One of them was Jefferson Davis, then a US senator from Mississippi and later the president of the Confederate States of America. At the time, Davis was serving as chairman of the Senate Committee of Military Affairs. In that capacity he had been an advocate of importing camels for military use, but he wasn't able to do anything about it until 1852, when he was appointed secretary of war. This gave him the authority, but not all the support, he needed. It took another three years before he was able to convince Congress that it was an experiment worth trying. On March 3, 1855, the lawmakers appropriated thirty thousand dollars for the project, and the US Camel Corps became a reality. On paper, at least.

First the army had to get some camels. This was no easy task, considering that there weren't any left in North America, and the nearest camel outlets appeared to be Africa and the Middle East. Undaunted, the army ordered Wayne and Lt. David Porter aboard the troop ship USS *Supply* and they shipped out of New York on June 3, 1855, headed for North Africa. They made their first buy in Tunisia but, because of inexperience, didn't recognize that their purchase had medical problems that made him unfit for military duty. Buying healthy camels apparently wasn't easy. Many of the good ones were involved in the war in the Crimea, carrying troops and supplies to the various fronts. They left Africa and sailed for Malta, Greece, and Turkey, looking for camels but without success. They were, however, learning about camels. The experience taught them that one-humped Arabian camels were best for riding, while the two-humped Bactrians were better pack animals. They also learned how to detect the sick animals that unscrupulous camel dealers tried to sell them.

The two procurers finally returned to North Africa and found a plentiful supply in Egypt. But there were more obstacles to overcome. Egyptian government regulations wouldn't allow them to take the camels out of the country. Under-the-table payments and outright bribes eventually took care of the problem, and the USS *Supply* left Egypt with a cargo that included thirty-three camels and five camel drovers. The drovers were hired to care for the animals during the two-month trip back to the United States, and to educate the American soldiers about their idiosyncrasies and unfamiliar habits once they got on American soil. One of the camels died en route, but two babies were born. When the ship arrived at Indianola, Texas, they unloaded thirty-four of the creatures.

After they were given several weeks of rest, the camels were moved to Camp Verde, about sixty miles west of San Antonio. Once there the beasts were put to little use other than carrying supplies from town. Although Wayne sent continual reports to Davis back in Washington, DC, about the camels' progress, the two had a falling out over whether or not to breed the animals. Wayne favored the experiment; Davis was against it. Wayne eventually asked for a transfer, and the Camel Corps underwent a series of leadership changes until 1857.

Still trying to put the animals to good use, the army assigned them to a crew that had been ordered to survey unexplored territory between El Paso, Texas, and the Colorado River. The party was led by Lt. Edward Fitzgerald Beale and consisted of twenty-five camels, forty-four soldiers, numerous horses and mules, and two camel drovers, Greek George and Philip Tedro. After some initial problems, the camels performed well, often leading the crew over terrain that mules and horses could not easily maneuver. At one point the camels actually saved the expedition from disaster when their instruments failed them and they became lost. As water supplies ran dangerously low, the camels were able to lead the group to a river about twenty miles from camp. Beale was jubilant, and continued his mission, arriving at the Colorado River without further incident. But although the camels had won over the skeptics in the army, Washington was not convinced. This did not bode well for the Camel Corps, and things got even worse when the hierarchy changed.

James Buchanan was elected president in 1856, and one of his first moves was to replace Davis with John B. Floyd as secretary of war. This led to some bitter infighting between Floyd and Maj. Gen. David Twiggs, his army commander in Texas. Floyd was a proponent of the Camel Corps; Twiggs hated the animals. He was outraged when he found out that part of his command was a herd of camels. His hatred was so intense that he sent a steady stream of complaints to his superior about the creatures that he called "smelly and rotten."

Twiggs had a lot of support among his men. Those ordered to work with the camels claimed they were bad tempered, spit a lot, held grudges, frequently refused to follow orders, and often kicked them. And, they said, the camels stunk. They smelled so bad, the handlers maintained, that they not only offended the olfactory senses of the humans but also caused panic and stampeding among the domesticated livestock at the camp. There were other complaints that carried even more weight. Although the camels performed well when called upon to serve, they were used only sparingly. They carried supplies once in a while, and made infrequent surveying trips. Outside of that, they spent their time confined to their specially built pens, where they were seen as an increasing financial drain on the military. The end was near. Eight years after it started, the noble experiment was about to end.

The prospect of civil war was looming in Washington, railroads were crossing the land, and the camels billeted in the deserts of the Southwest became matters of little or no concern. When the war broke out, the camels stationed in Texas became part of the Confederacy, but the rebel forces likewise had very little use for them. After the war, they were auctioned off, but some were reclaimed as stolen property by the federal government, which then released them into the desert. Other veterans of the failed campaign were sold to zoos, circuses, mining companies, and prospectors. A few entrepreneurs tried to use them in mail delivery ventures; others started long-range hauling operations. None lasted long. Beale showed some mercy toward the beasts of burden, allowing his camels to live out their lives on his ranch in California.

Philip Tedro was one of the entrepreneurs. He knew camels. He was one of the drovers brought to this country with the original herd, and when Beale and Porter were transferred to posts in the eastern United States, he was one of the few experts left to oversee the camels. So if anyone could use them to make an operation successful, he was the man.

By this time Tedro was well-known in the deserts of Arizona and California, but nobody knew him by that name. He was of Greek-Syrian origin and his real name was Philip Tedro, but he changed it to Hadji Ali when he converted to Islam. After arriving in the United States, he underwent another name change, this time to Hi Jolly. The oft-stated reason was that the soldiers with whom he was serving either had difficulty pronouncing his name or were too lazy to learn the correct pronunciation, and had shortened it to Hi Jolly. The name stuck.

When the camel experiment withered and died, Hi Jolly bought some of the beasts and established a freight line between Yuma and Tucson. Although the camels were well-suited to the task of hauling huge loads across the arid sands, Jolly wasn't suited to life as a businessman. The venture failed. In 1868 he turned his last camel loose near Gila Bend and went to work for the army as a packer and scout at Fort McDowell near Phoenix. He became an American citizen in 1880 and reverted back to his original name of Philip Tedro when he signed the papers. He married later that year, and the union produced two children before Tedro (or Ali, or Jolly) abandoned his family and went prospecting for gold.

He was a familiar figure, an old desert rat who hung around the barren areas on both sides of the Colorado River. He died in 1902, but his name lives on. Now the town of Quartzsite, on the Arizona side of the river, holds Hi Jolly Days every year, and camels are the festival's theme. His grave site in the local cemetery is a stone pyramid topped by a copper silhouette of a camel, erected by the State of Arizona in 1935 to commemorate his contributions to the settlement of the territory. It is now the town's most popular tourist attraction.

Questions still arise, however, about Hi Jolly's connection to the Red Ghost. There are two probable answers. The first is that the Red Ghost may have been one of the camels he tended years before. The second is more appealing to the storytellers.

According to the tales that survive him, the old drover perished when he went out into the desert to find a wild camel that had been terrorizing the area. When they found his body, it was lying next to that of a dead camel, with one of his arms wrapped around the beast's neck. To this day no one can substantiate the story, but it is told and retold every year. With every retelling there is also included some further supposition that the dead camel was the Red Ghost.

Those tales are, geographically at least, in direct contradiction to most other stories dealing with the mysterious creature. Hi Jolly lived in western Arizona; all the other alleged sightings occurred near the eastern border. However, for years after the dissolution of the Camel Corps, the animals wandered freely across the entire Southwest. Those released by the army were joined by some that were set loose by mining companies in San Francisco and British Columbia. These herds drifted as far south as Nevada. The ex-army beasts roamed across Texas, California, and Arizona, so camel sightings were nothing out of the ordinary. But the Red Ghost was different, and those who claimed to have seen him recounted their stories with both anger and fear, even while creating a myth.

Shortly after the incident involving the miners at Eagle Creek, a rancher reported seeing the Red Ghost carrying a rider who didn't appear to be alive. The rider's arms flailed wildly as the camel tore through the countryside, as if he was signaling for help. A prospector swore he saw the beast kill and eat a full-size brown bear. Another claimed he chased it and saw it disappear before his eyes. By this time, the Red Ghost tales were a definite part of Arizona lore. Even the Hispanic population had adopted him as part of their culture, and referred to him as *fantasia colorado*.

The stories increased in direct proportion to the ghastliness of it all. Cyrus Hamblin, a rancher who owned a spread near the Salt River about eighty miles northwest of Eagle Creek, was out looking for strays when he climbed to the top of a small ridge to get a better view. He didn't spot any cattle from his perch, but he did see what he thought was a camel. He stayed in the hope of getting a better look. Eventually the camel walked into an open space and what Hamlin saw made him a believer. The lump on the camel's back was larger than usual because it was covered with the body of a man. When Hamlin told what he had seen, the skepticism was greatly reduced. Hamlin had spent several years in the area, so he was familiar with the heat of the desert and the tricks it can play. His reputation was widely that of a man who could be trusted. His account was generally accepted as the truth. But if there was a need for more verification, another episode in the story of the Red Ghost soon made Hamlin's version undeniable.

Shortly afterwards, the Red Ghost was spotted in the Verde Valley, nearly sixty miles northwest of Hamlin's spread. This time, a group of prospectors not only saw the camel but were able to get close enough to take a few rifle shots at it. They missed, but the gunfire frightened the animal and it rapidly moved away into the thick undergrowth. As it fled, something fell from its back and rolled away. The miners eagerly retrieved it. The object was a human skull. A skull with shreds of flesh and hair still attached to it. Now there could be no doubt that there was such a creature as the Red Ghost, but also that the unearthly apparition was carrying a headless rider. Word of this gruesome discovery spread like the proverbial wildfire throughout the territory, assisted by a small minority of frontier newspaper editors who frequently ignored the facts that stood in the way of a good story.

A few days later, also in the Verde River area, a wagon train was bedded down for the night when "a great beast" flapped down on their camp on black wings, then landed with such force that it jarred the ground and knocked over two wagons. Terrified, the freighters scattered and stayed away until morning. When they got their courage back and returned to camp, they found prints of huge, cloven hoofs and red hairs sticking to one of the overturned wagons. Their Red Ghost story was met with renewed skepticism, however, primarily because their cargo contained several kegs of whiskey.

The phantom then made its ghostly way to the Phoenix area, where the last violent encounter was reported. A cowhand working on a ranch east of the city claimed he had roped a camel he found skulking about a corral. Once caught in the noose, the camel charged the cowboy's horse. The impact knocked both horse and rider to the ground. As the beast passed over them, the cowboy said, he observed that the creature was carrying a skeleton on its back. There were other sightings, but none mentioned the camel's human cargo.

The stories, and the terror they produced, continued until 1893 when Mizoo Hastings, an eastern Arizona farmer, spotted a huge red camel grazing in his vegetable patch. Hastings downed the animal with one shot. When he examined the corpse, it still bore the leather straps that once could have been used to tie a human to its back. The *Mohave County Miner* published this eulogy:

Another ghost is laid. Another of the tribe of gaunt hob-goblins that keep the romance of the mysterious southern deserts is gone. Another of the unearthly dangers that the timid Mexican women used to pray against has departed.

Mizoo Hastings of Ore was the priest that exorcised this phantom. Mizoo has a ranch a little above the gold camp on the San Francisco River. He woke up one morning and saw through the window of his cabin a big red camel banqueting in his turnip patch. Mizoo took a dead rest on the window sill and blazed away. He got the camel.

When he went out to examine the beast, he found that he was all scarred up and had evidently had a very hard time. He was covered with a perfect network of knotted rawhide strips. They had been on him so long that some of the strands had cut their way into the flesh.

If there actually was a body strapped to the camel, no one is certain how it got there. But, of course, there was speculation.

Hi Jolly's grave marker in Quartzsite is associated with the Red Ghost.

One theory blamed it on a practical joke gone bad. According to that version, a group of soldiers strapped a young recruit to the camel's hump as part of an initiation rite. But something spooked the camel and it took off into the wilderness with its unwilling passenger securely tied to its back. The soldiers tried to catch it but never did. They then swore each other to secrecy. The truth, if there was any involved, never came out.

Another speculated that a drover got lost in the desert and strapped himself to his camel's back in the vain hope that it would find water. If it did, it was too late, and the lost drover, too weak to free himself, became the headless rider.

Regardless, there were no more Red Ghost sightings after Mizoo Hastings dispatched the turnip eater in his garden. But other camels made occasional appearances for several years afterwards. The last authenticated sighting was reported in 1901 when a survey crew working the Arizona-Mexico border claimed they had seen a herd. But others continued for several more years. A railroad crew said they spotted one near Wickenburg in 1913; a camel allegedly caused a horse stampede near Banning, California, in 1929; and in 1941, persons unnamed said they saw one near California's Salton Sea.

TERESA URREA: THE WOMAN WHO HEALED

Clifton Cemetery rests quietly on the slopes along Ward Canyon Road, a winding stretch of pavement that twists its way through the copper-toned hills southeast of Clifton. It is a lonely place. Two cypress trees rise from the barren surroundings in open defiance of the sun that scorches the land more than three hundred days a year. Not many go there now. The cemetery is old and almost filled to capacity, so there's little room for new graves. Creosote bushes have established small stands on some of the plots, but others are well-tended to honor those buried there.

There was a time, more than a century ago, when visitors numbered in the hundreds. Most of them came to pay homage to their beloved Teresa Urrea, whom they considered a saint. Today the crowds that search for Teresa Urrea have diminished, almost down to nothing. A scant few, never more than two or three people at a time, make the occasional journey to search for her grave. But unless they know exactly what they're looking for, they probably don't find what they seek. The grave is unmarked. It is one of several in the hallowed ground surrounded by a wrought-iron picket fence with no granite headstone, no wooden marker, and no other designation about whose remains lie there. Only a concrete slab covering the grave sets it apart from the others.

Some claim they know which grave is hers, but they are reluctant to point it out. Perhaps they're not sure of the exact location. Perhaps they don't want people flocking to the cemetery and disturbing the solitude that hovers over the sacred ground. They have their reasons, spoken or not.

Although her grave site is an uncertainty, Teresa Urrea's short life actually did end in Clifton, on January 11, 1906. She was thirty-three years old, a victim of pulmonary consumption. According to some, she asked to be buried next to her father, the same father who had disowned her years earlier because she had gone against his wishes. That may be hearsay. But then much of her life story is hearsay.

During her brief time on earth, she was referred to as a faith healer, revolutionary, scam artist, heretic, common criminal, the New World's Joan of Arc, heroine, fraud, spiritual leader, and rabble-rouser. She was revered by many, used by several, and exploited by a few. Thousands believed she could heal the sick; thousands took up her name in a rebel cause. Very little of this was of her own doing.

All the stories, all the claims, all the allegations had their beginnings on October 15, 1873, when Teresa Urrea was born on a ranch north of Ocoroni in the state of Sinaloa, Mexico. She was named Teresa but usually called Teresita, and she was illegitimate. Her father was don Tomas Urrea, a wealthy landowner who sired seventeen other children with a variety of women. Her mother was Cayetana Chavez, a fourteen-year-old Yaqui Indian who worked on one of the don's ranches. Cayetana also had four other children of uncertain paternity.

For her first fourteen years, Teresa had no knowledge of her father. Because don Tomas was an important political figure, her mother raised the child away from the Urrea household, keeping her true identity a secret. Then her mother disappeared, leaving Teresa to be raised by an aunt. In 1888 she was moved to her father's ranch in Cabora, where she met Maria Sonora, another of her father's servants, who taught her the use of herbs to cure certain illnesses. During that time, her father learned of her relationship to him and took her into his immediate family. Life was good then. She studied music and consorted with his political allies, including Lauro Aguirre, a newspaperman and engineer with strong antigovernment views.

When Teresa matured, don Tomas apprenticed her to a *curandera* (healer) named Huila, who recognized that the girl had healing gifts. Not only that, the elderly woman claimed, Teresa was also a clairvoyant who could calm patients in extreme pain merely by looking them in the eyes. Huila served as a midwife to Indians of the region. She took the young Teresita on her rounds and swore that the girl could put a woman in labor into a trance, making the birth painless. Huila also introduced her to a Yaqui medicine man who taught her the uses of herbs, plants, and cacti as instruments of healing. Teresa was a good student. She retained everything she learned from Huila and the medicine man, and would put the knowledge to use in her later years.

But just as her life took this turn for the better, Teresa fell into a catatonic shock, allegedly brought on by a rape attempt.

When she was discovered, her body was rigid, in a seizure so severe that not even Huila could bring her out of it. She then lapsed into a coma. After twelve days, don Tomas ordered his ranch hands to build a coffin. On the thirteenth day, Teresa apparently died. She was examined by Huila, don Tomas, and a doctor from a neighboring village. They found no pulse; she was cold and not breathing. The servants bathed her, wrapped her in a white burial dress, and placed a rosary around her hands. That night, as they prayed over her body, Teresa sat up and asked why everyone was so sad. After assuring them that she was not dead, she then lapsed into an unconscious state that lasted more than three months. The episode changed her life forever. When fully recovered, she began experiencing trances and, in them, she claimed, the Virgin Mary instructed her to heal the sick and injured.

And so it began.

Some of her earlier cures were spectacular in themselves, but grew to mythical proportions when repeated by those around her and those she cured. In one case she gave audience to a young farmhand who had been kicked in the head by a mule. She picked up a handful of soil, spit into it, and wiped the mud on the man's wound. Those who witnessed the event said he was instantly healed. News of her curative powers spread. As the stories grew, so did her band of followers. The stream of devotees coming to the ranch grew steadily. The roads leading to her father's ranch were filled with those hoping to be cured. Teresa obliged. She turned no one away and never requested payment of any kind from those she cured.

This created a hardship for don Tomas because it meant he had to dig new wells, hire extra help, and lay in supplies to deal with the faithful, who were coming in crowds as large as five thousand per day. Among them were large numbers of Christianized Indians—Yaquis and Mayos from Sonora, the Gusaves from Sinaloa, and the Tomochitecos and Tarahumaras from Chihuahua. Most were barefoot, but they walked for miles across the harsh landscape to visit the young woman who had become a living idol. Many of them had been forced off their land by the government, a factor that would later play a key role in the legend of Teresa Urrea.

The Indians were soon followed by Mexicans, then Americans. Inevitably, newspaper and magazine reporters also began showing up, lured by the prospect of a good story. Teresa was soon an international celebrity featured in articles that appeared in the *New York Times, San Francisco Daily Examiner, Los Angeles Times,* and *Overland Monthly.*

The trouble started about the same time. The Indians held her in awe, but her reputation was becoming a cause of great concern for the Mexican government and the Catholic Church. Members of the Tomochiteco tribe were so impressed after she cured one of their warriors of a tumor that they proclaimed her "Santa Teresa," and installed her as their village saint. They carved an image of her out of native wood and placed it in the mission church, right next to the statues of Jesus and the Virgin Mary. This bordered on heresy and it did not sit well with the missionaries who had spent years converting the natives. The circuit-riding priest in charge of maintaining Catholicism among the tribes came into Tomochic and flew into a rage when he found the wooden idol. Already troubled by her growing fame, he sent a message to the Vatican, then telegraphed Mexican President Porfirio Díaz and requested federal intervention. Almost simultaneously, government spies also sent Díaz a telegram, asserting that Teresa was preaching liberation to the tribes.

Some of the allegations were true. Teresa preached justice to the tribes that had been subjected to genocidal wars, land seizures, and forced relocation. After the federal troops hanged a three-year-old boy from a tree, she denounced the government's tactic in a written statement: "Do you wonder why the tribe fights the forces of such a government? My poor Indians! They are the bravest and most persecuted people on earth! They will fight for their rights until they win or are exterminated. God help them! There are few of them left."

It was a time directly headed toward revolution. In situations like that, there arises a cause, and a cause needs a leader. Unfortunately for her, the Tomochitecos assigned that role to Teresa Urrea. At the same time, the federal government, under direct orders from President Díaz, moved to put down a rebellion by the Tomochitecos. Díaz was deeply troubled by the influence that the young woman apparently had over the tribe, ignoring the fact that she neither asked for nor wanted such power. Those who fought back had adopted the battle cry of "Viva de Santa de Cabora!" and they were ferocious in their resistance; this also was attributed to Teresa, although she had nothing to do with it. To make matters worse, the Indians openly sought her blessing for a series of revolts over land boundaries. She refused, but inadvertently gave tacit support to the cause when she reportedly told the rebels that "God intended for you to have the lands, or He would not have given them to you."

In 1891 an armed rebel group holed up in a village after fighting a government force. The Federales encircled the village and burned it to the ground. Women and children who took refuge in the church met fiery deaths in an incident so horrible that other revolutionaries took up the battle cry and began calling themselves Teresistas.

Díaz was so threatened that he had to take action. Fearful of losing his power over the tribes, he denounced Teresa as "the most dangerous girl in Mexico," and sent her and her father into exile in 1892. Although there was no evidence that might have convicted them of anything resembling treason, they were shipped by railroad to Nogales, Arizona Territory, and ordered never to return.

And the legend grew. All along the railroad line, Indian warriors on foot and horseback raised their weapons in salute as the train passed.

The action was sensationalized and distorted by the press, and drew conflicting reports all across Mexico and the United States. On June 16, 1892, the *New York Times* carried a front page story headlined "A Saint to Be Shot." The story, datelined San Antonio, Texas, declared that a businessman who had recently returned from Guaymas, Sonora, said that "the wildest excitement exists among the ignorant classes of Mexicans throughout the state of Sonora over the arrest and conviction of Teresa Urrea, the celebrated saint of Cacheora.... St. Teresa was arrested three weeks ago by a detachment of soldiers, who escorted her and her aged father, Thomas Urrea, to Guaymas. Both were heavily ironed and were kept closely confined in prison until placed on trial."

According to the story, the judge found both guilty of witchery. Teresa was sentenced to be shot and her father imprisoned for life. The report also noted that "[she] is possessed of some strange power [and] the judge firmly believes that she is a witch," then concluded that "she awaits her fate quietly and offered no defense when on trial."

But the June 28, 1892, edition of the *Times* printed somewhat of a retraction by announcing, again on the front page, that "the reported execution of the celebrated Teresa Urrea, the 'Saint of Socorro,' some days ago is untrue. The story was purposely circulated by the Mexican authorities in order to quell the excitement among the restless Indians, who were becoming dangerous and flocking to Nogales in great numbers to see their patron saint and receive her wonderful treatment for all diseases."

What happened, the *Times* explained, was that Teresa did attempt to return to her former home in Mexico but was intercepted by the police, who issued the false report about her death. The article ended with, "She was again transported to the United States border and warned that if she ventured into Mexico again, she would be put to death."

Although she apparently agreed to the terms of her exile, the controversy didn't end. The thousands of pilgrims who flocked to Nogales to see her became recruitment prospects for the revolutionaries, who were now openly plotting to overthrow the Díaz government. The never-ending pressure to become actively involved became too much for Teresa; she and her father left Nogales and relocated in Solomonville in eastern Arizona Territory in 1895.

A year later they moved to El Paso, Texas, but that city was too close to the Mexican border. The harassment continued. After surviving three assassination attempts, Teresa still refused to take sides in the ongoing conflicts and even made a rare statement to the *El Paso Herald*, saying, "I have noticed with much pain that the persons who have taken up arms in Mexican territory have invoked my name in aid of the schemes they are carrying through. But I repeat I am not one who authorizes or at the same time interferes with these proceedings."

The declaration had little effect. Rebels led by Lauro Aguirre attacked a customs house in Nogales. Fourteen people from both sides were slain. Some of the dead revolutionaries had photographs of Teresa Urrea pinned to their clothing, and the government used that to further the anti-Teresa campaign. One of the survivors was taken to court, where he blamed Lauro Aguirre and Teresa's father, don Tomas, for much of the trouble, because "the girl does as he [Aguirre] wants her to." Aguirre was at that time publishing *El Independiente*, a Texas newspaper, and Teresa was writing columns for the publication. Aguirre spread her fame through his writing, but she refused him when he asked her to join him in his plans to launch a full-scale revolution. Then on August 13, 1896, Aguirre led the armed revolt and blew up the customs house. Teresa was stunned.

In its report of the incident, the August 20, 1896, edition of the *New York Times* observed, "Aguirre is the worst, they say, as he has complete control over Teresa's father. . . . [He] is a highly educated man in his language but is said to be dissipated. It is estimated by the Mexican officials here that he and Santa Teresa, by their influence, have caused the death of more than 1,000 people in the last six or seven years."

This episode fueled the Mexican government's intense hatred for Teresa and her father. The beleaguered duo was forced to leave El Paso and settle in Clifton, a mining community in eastern Arizona Territory. She continued to minister to the sick and poor, and her reputation continued to grow. One story said that when her curing powers occurred, the chemistry of her body changed and her perspiration had an aroma similar to perfume. Another folktale recounted that her helpers were selling her bathwater as a miraculous cure-all. At that same time, the *Los Angeles Times* observed that "this exiled 'saint' seems to be the embodiment of simplicity, and to look into her mysterious dark eyes one would never think her capable of instigating an insurrection."

But if newspaper reports of that era were to be considered the truth and nothing but the truth, Teresa did make at least one more trip into Mexico. The January 29, 1898, edition of *L'abeille de la Nouvelle Orleans* reported that she had returned to her native country after "a brief sojourn" in Arizona. The story read, in part: "Reports have reached Hermosilla that she is among the Yaqui Indians, exerting her wonderful influences to stir them up to go on the warpath. About 200 braves have allied themselves to her fanatical cause and a raid is threatened at any time. . . . She has incited three small revolutions on the border against the Mexican government and has been the cause of much bloodshed."

Once again, Teresa was forced to make public denials of her involvement while trying to lead what, for her, was a normal life.

Despite her notoriety, she might have found serenity if fate hadn't intervened once more.

It happened in 1900 when the Saint of Cabora turned uncharacteristically commercial. She hooked up with a medical company in New York on what was billed as "a nationwide curing crusade." The company offered her ten thousand dollars and she accepted on the condition that none of her patients would be charged for her help. Under terms of the contract, she left Clifton and moved to California, where she appeared to be an instant success. A December 1902 edition of the *Los Angeles Times* carried a report that said, in part: "The halt, the blind, the inwardly distressed, paralytics almost helpless and others ravaged by consumption, are helped to her doors each day by friends and relatives and none go there without the belief that by laying on of her magic hands they will be cured. . . . Santa Teresa has great power over the Yaquis, from whose country she sprang, and has been the subject of many fantastic stories based more or less on fact. In some ways, her influence is really remarkable."

But all was not well. She discovered that her partners in the venture were nothing more than snake-oil merchants who, despite the promises made in the contract, were collecting exorbitant fees from her followers. Disillusioned and disheartened, Teresa found a lawyer who got her out of the contract, and she returned to Clifton.

Not to a happy ending, however.

Back home, she and her father had a major falling-out over her choice of husbands. She wanted to marry Guadalupe Rodriguez, a mine worker. Don Tomas forbade the union. She married him anyway. The marriage lasted less than one day. Her new husband pulled a gun and marched her into the surrounding desert, where he shot her. She had refused to go to Mexico with him. His aim was faulty, however, and Teresa suffered only a flesh wound. She fled and the townspeople soon captured Rodriguez. He was tried, judged insane, and sentenced to an asylum.

Things did get better after that, but only for a while. She married John Van Order, and the couple had two daughters: Laura, born in 1902, and Magdelena, born in 1904. But a blissful life was not in her future. Shortly after the second birth, Teresa's health began to fail. Her followers said she had given away too much of her soul while healing the sick and injured. She opened a small clinic where she continued to practice her brand of medicine. When a major flood threatened to inundate Clifton, she was among those who spent freezing nights filling and stacking sandbags. All that activity took a toll on Teresa, and she was diagnosed with pulmonary tuberculosis in 1905. Although too weak to stand, she continued to bless all those who came to see her almost up to the time of her death.

A large gathering of followers attended her funeral. Without their beloved saint preaching to them and healing them, however, they eventually found other pursuits. Over time, fewer and fewer people remembered her. For the next eighty years, the story of Teresa Urrea lay dormant along with her remains in an untended cemetery where the sun is the only constant and where an occasional rainfall reshapes the landscape while imperiling the graves.

It might have stayed that way except for the interest of Luis Perez, a professor from Silver City, New Mexico, who was considered one of the greatest living authorities on the legend of Teresita.

According to a story published in the March 25, 1996, edition of the *Arizona Republic*, Perez had heard the stories about the lost grave and came to Clifton determined to find it. He discovered an old photograph of a painting that showed her burial plot. By matching landmarks, he established what is now considered the official grave site. The discovery, made in 1993, brought about another minor miracle, according to Walter Mares, a Clifton newspaper publisher and a member of the Clifton Chamber of Commerce.

Mares said that in 1994, the Clifton Town Council had appointed a graveyard sexton and gave him the manpower to clean up the cemetery, which had been sorely neglected for several years. Volunteers helped with the restoration, and for the first time in decades, the burial ground became a place to go and reflect, not just an area to be visited in time of sorrow. "When you have trials

Teresa Urrea rests in an unmarked grave in the Clifton Cemetery.

and tribulations and there is so much tumult, the peace of Teresita is beyond description," Mares said.

It wasn't the same adulation that had been bestowed upon her a century before, but there was a brief resurgence of Teresita fervor. City officials announced plans to build a small shrine next to her grave site. Next, the town established an annual Fiesta de la Santa de Cabora, a daylong celebration that included a pilgrimage to her grave site, music, food, art shows, and dancers. The excitement didn't endure, however. Within a decade, economics and local politics forced cancellation of the festival; the shrine never got beyond the planning stage.

Today the sun rises and sets over an unmarked grave where only a few determined visitors come to visit what may be the grave of Teresa Urrea, the Saint of Cabora.

MYSTERIOUS GRAND CANYON DEATHS

The Grand Canyon is in a state of constant realignment. The changes are subtle, almost unnoticed by the human eye because they occur not in mere days or weeks but over the millennia. It's been that way for more than six million years, ever since the Colorado River and other forces of nature began carving the wandering gorge into the plateaus of northern Arizona.

The canyon is a spectacular sight, one of the Seven Natural Wonders of the World, and it attracts more than five million visitors every year. But its scenic beauty conceals a dark side. Hundreds, if not thousands, of people have been injured or lost their lives in its depths. Because it has been there for so long, there are no exact figures on how many deaths have occurred on the trails, side canyons, and the river that runs through it, but since the 1880s, when people first started keeping track of such things, there have been at least six hundred recorded fatalities. Most of them are single episodes in which death is caused by overexertion, falling, drowning, suicide, and even murder.

The largest toll—240 deaths between 1956 and 2003—came from aircraft accidents. In 1956 a TWA Lockheed Super Constellation and a United Airlines Douglas DC7 collided over the canyon, killing everyone on board both planes, a total of 128 victims. Thirty years later, twenty-five people died when a helicopter rose from below the canyon rim and smashed into a twin-engine airplane. Eight more tourists died when a sightseeing plane lost an engine and crashed in 1995. Helicopter crashes in 2001 and 2003 resulted in another thirteen deaths.

In almost all the other cases—the twenty-three murders, the fifty suicides, the eighty drownings—the bodies have been recovered and grieving relatives given closure. But nobody knows, and probably nobody ever will know, what happened to adventurers Glen and Bessie Hyde, and explorers O. G. Howland, Seneca Howland, and William Dunn. They all disappeared under mysterious circumstances, their bodies were never found, and their fates are still being debated almost 150 years later.

The case of Glen and Bessie Hyde is the most intriguing, and still attracts considerable attention, primarily because it keeps getting solved and unsolved. But the young couple's disappearance in 1928 was not the first involving would-be canyon conquerors.

Nearly sixty years earlier, in 1869, Maj. John Wesley Powell and a small band of brave and intrepid companions set out to be the first on record to explore the entire 277 miles of the canyon by raft. Powell, a one-armed Civil War veteran, and his party of eight were under the sponsorship of the Smithsonian Institution; their goal was to map the river, make contact with Native American tribes, and record geological data. Their ten-month journey would take them into uncharted areas and unknown peril, even though they already had some concept of the roaring waters that awaited them.

The group divided themselves, their rations, tools, instruments, and other necessities, among three sturdy, handcrafted boats that were specifically built to withstand the rapids along the Colorado. Their instruments and supplies were stored in watertight cabins in case any of the boats were caught in the swirling waters and capsized.

Despite all the extra precautions and reinforcements, the boats were a far cry from the well-equipped, almost unsinkable, multipassenger motorized rafts that carry tourists along the river today. And they encountered many hardships because, although they were very well prepared, the crew endured many dunkings, which meant they had to halt their journey to dry out supplies, repair broken equipment, and find new wood for the oars they lost. Powell kept meticulous journals in which he described the hardships of the rugged land and untamed water, as well as vivid descriptions of the canyon's natural beauty.

But the rigors of the journey eventually became too much for some members of the expedition. On the evening of August 27, 1869, three of them approached Powell and said they'd had enough. They were leaving. They were still at least forty-five miles from where the trek was supposed to end, but that made little or no difference. The three men—Capt. O. G. Howland, his brother Seneca, and William Dunn—were determined. They figured they could scramble up to the south rim of the canyon then make contact with either Mormon settlements or Native American villages for supplies and directions back to civilization.

Powell tried to talk them out of leaving and urged them to stay with the group. He warned that the climb out of the canyon was dangerous and that the nearest Mormon settlement was at least seventy-five miles away even if they did get to the top. Seneca Howland weakened and tried to convince the other two that it was too dangerous, but his argument had no impact. The trio left camp that morning, carrying with them letters and mementos from the others, and a copy of the expedition journal which Powell had kept in duplicate. They were never seen or heard from again.

Powell and his remaining crew of five returned to the river and got through the next set of rapids in a few minutes. They beached their boats and fired a shot to signal that they had made it through, hoping that the other three would come back. After a lengthy wait and no response, they resumed their journey without them.

No one was, or is, certain what happened. The most common speculation was that they did reach the canyon rim only to be killed by Indians who mistook them for some miners who had raped a young tribal maiden. A second, but less popular, theory was that white settlers killed them because they were considered interlopers.

The mystery took on a bit of added meaning in 1939 when the white water where the trio left the main group was named Separation Rapid, and a plaque was placed at the site to honor their memory. The memorial had a short life, however. It is now covered by the eastern end of Lake Mead.

Ninety-five days after they started, Powell and the five men who toughed it out with him emerged from the wilderness with maps, fossils, sketches, and other information that would prove invaluable to those who would follow. Powell later was appointed head of the US Geological Survey, and the book he wrote about the journey is still ranked as one of the classics of exploration.

Glen and Bessie Hyde had a similar vision when they set out to explore and conquer the Grand Canyon in 1928.

They were young newlyweds, restless and looking for adventure. Their plan was to traverse the wild waters of the Colorado River with the twin goals of setting a speed record for the journey and having Bessie become the first woman to run the river through the entire canyon. If they were successful, they reasoned, there'd be a book deal, the lecture circuit, and, potentially, a series of reenactments on the vaudeville stage.

Glen had some experience as a river runner; he had taken already raft trips down Idaho's Salmon and Snake Rivers. But Bessie was a novice. Only twenty-two at the time, she had led a rather full life prior to hooking up with Glen Hyde. She was born in Maryland and raised in West Virginia as Bessie Haley, married when she was twenty, divorced when she was twenty-two, remarried at twenty-two. She attended Marshall College and married Earl Helmick, a high school classmate, in Catlettsburg, Kentucky, in 1926. The couple lived together for only a couple of months before Bessie returned to her parents' home in West Virginia, then left to study art in San Francisco.

That career move didn't last much longer than her marriage. In 1927 she left San Francisco aboard a steamship headed for Los Angeles. En route, she met Glen Hyde and they began a shipboard romance that blossomed into true love and a marriage proposal. But Bessie was still married to Helmick, and he refused to agree to a divorce. The young lovers found an easy solution—Bessie moved to

Elko, Nevada, established the required residency, and got a divorce decree on April 11, 1928. She married Glen Hyde the next day.

Hyde considered himself an adventurer who was stuck in a humdrum life. He was born near Spokane, Washington, in 1898 and lived there until he was twelve, when the family moved to California. He ended his schooling after a short time in college and moved to Idaho, where he worked on a family farm. He and his new wife returned to the farm but soon decided there was more to life than milking cows and shoveling manure. At the end of summer in 1928, they decided it was time to take a delayed honeymoon. Their destination would be the Grand Canyon, where they would make a boat trip through the rapids in a bulky watercraft that Hyde had built. Their plans drew some attention from local newspapers. A year later, the same newspapers would be filled with stories about them, but they would not be success stories.

The couple started their journey in Utah on the Green River. Their craft was a flat-bottomed wooden sweep scow that weighed two tons. Despite its weight, the scow was of a type commonly used for river rafting at the time. And there was also a rather dangerous custom among rafters—they didn't wear life preservers or jackets. The boats didn't even carry such precautionary equipment. This factor may or may not have played a role in what would eventually happen.

The Hydes set out in October and things went well at first. Photographers documented portions of their trip, and the young honeymooners sent upbeat messages back to their families, reporting that they were making remarkable progress and were ahead of schedule. Bessie also kept a detailed journal, mentioning every rapid and twist in the river, as well as the emotions they felt while traversing them. They floated through canyons that already had names and some that didn't. They reached Glen Canyon and Lees Ferry by early November, again ahead of schedule and, according to one message Glen sent his father, it was "great sport."

They rested at Lees Ferry for a while, talked with some of the locals, and were given well-intended advice to abandon their quest. Jeremiah Johnson, whose father had died on the river, warned them that "they were playing with death." Owen Clark, a government employee, also cautioned them about taking a woman along on a trek that had been accomplished only a few times before, and always by men. But, he also noted, Hyde appeared competent, and added "it was surprising the way he could handle that boat."

As the Grand Canyon narrowed beyond Lees Ferry, the river became swifter and the rapids grew worse, but the pair didn't relent. They arrived at Bright Angel Creek in mid-November. They tied up their cumbersome scow and hiked up the South Kaibab Trail to the canyon's south rim. They rested there for a while, then gathered up the supplies they needed for the remainder of their journey. They then met Emery Kolb, the legendary Grand Canyon photographer. He drove them around the South Rim, treated them to lunch, and, at their request, snapped a couple of shots of them as they stood at the canyon's edge. Kolb told them they could pick up the photos on their return trip, and the Hydes assured him they'd be back for them. They also met with newspaper reporters whose accounts were published as far away as New York. Shortly before their departure, they wrote what would be their final letters to relatives and friends. Both letters were filled with optimism and hope.

It was November 16 when they put their boat back into the Colorado, along with an unexpected guest. Adolph Gilbert Sutro, a wealthy adventurer who had once set speed and distance records with an airplane, asked if he might ride along for a few miles. The Hydes agreed. Unfortunately for Sutro, he had inadvertently hooked up with the duo as they were about to encounter some of the roughest water on the river. After two days and seven miles with them, Sutro relied on his philosophy that "it's better to be a live coward than a dead hero," and left the couple at Hermit Camp. While they were together, however, he took several photographs of the pair, which now appear regularly on Internet sites dealing with the Hydes. He was also perhaps the last person to see them alive.

On November 18 Sutro watched as the ambitious pair slipped back into the water. They were never seen again.

Hyde had earlier messaged his father to expect a telegram from Needles, California, on December 9, which would have been the last day of their journey as well as Hyde's thirtieth birthday. When he heard nothing after three days, the elder Hyde drove to the Grand Canyon and organized a search party. Using a small airplane, the would-be rescuers spotted the boat in early December, but because it was at the bottom of the canyon, they couldn't reach it until Christmas Day. It was in excellent condition, sitting upright with forty-two notches carved into the gunwale, one for each day of the trip. Most of the supplies were intact. A camera and some film were undamaged. The searchers also found Glen's gun, hiking boots, and Bessie's journal. The last entry was dated November 30, 1928. It was a series of dashes and numbers, apparently an attempt to mark water patterns they had to deal with.

The search for Glen and Bessie went on for months with no more results. R. C. Hyde, Glen's father, made other trips to the canyon, but they also were fruitless. He continued his quest until his death in 1945.

By then the speculation and rumors were already firmly entrenched.

Investigators initially determined that the couple died in some sort of accident, probably drowned when their boat overturned. It was a solid presumption; at every one of their stops along the way, the Hydes had related horror stories about being swept overboard, sometimes several times a day, as they maneuvered through eddies and whirlpools bearing such names as Sockdolager, Labyrinth, and Cataract.

Glen's father told friends he believed they had problems with their boat, beached it, and attempted to walk out of the canyon but became lost and died in the surrounding woods. Extensive searches for their remains were also futile, however.

Other versions of what might have happened likewise were never proven, but they abounded anyway. One was that Glen Hyde was not an ideal husband. His obsession with becoming rich and famous turned him into some sort of brute who drove his wife beyond her abilities. That, coupled with the fact that the Hydes had been on the river for so long, caused marital problems that were exacerbated by the bullying tactics he deemed necessary to complete the voyage. According to this supposition, Bessie finally had enough. She snapped, turned on Glen with a knife, and inflicted mortal wounds. Then she hiked out of the canyon to begin a new life as a widow, using an assumed name.

But friends and relatives dismissed that theory on the grounds that Glen was too mild-mannered and was too much in love to ever treat Bessie in such a fashion.

A second, and much more believable, suggestion is based on that love. Some theorists believe that when the couple reached the vicious rapids at mile 232, Bessie was washed overboard by the force of the water. When Glen reached in to help her, he also was swept off the boat. With no one left on board to help them, both perished. That supposition meshes well with the one presented by the investigators.

Another romantic theory put forth was that the couple wanted to get away from the dullness of farm life and start a new existence as different people out in the golden West. So they pushed their scow up on the beach, hiked out of the canyon together, and allegedly lived happily ever after. Considering how determined the Hydes were to reap the riches of a successful excursion, however, this seems highly doubtful.

In his later years, Sutro remembered that Hyde seemed obsessed with how much money he and his wife could make if they successfully completed their journey. He also noted that Bessie was terrified and "registered stark fear." Those revelations, published after an interview with Sutro thirty years later, added fuel to the belief that Bessie might have turned on her husband out of fear for her own life.

Some also concluded that it was the other way around—Glen killed Bessie because she refused to continue the trip, thus dashing his hopes for life as a wealthy couple. After murdering her, he walked out of the canyon, took a different name, and lived out

Glen and Bessie Hyde posed for Emery Kolb before disappearing in the Grand Canyon.

the remainder of his life somewhere in the West. Emery Kolb gave that theory some support when he told an interviewer that Bessie seemed apprehensive about going on, and that she wondered if she'd "ever wear nice shoes again."

In one of the more ridiculous versions, Kolb himself becomes implicated in the mystery. According to some, Kolb felt so sorry for Bessie and her predicament that he killed Glen to save her from a violent death on the Colorado River. This theory got some major support in 1976. After Kolb's death that year, a skeleton was found in his garage with a bullet lodged in the skull. Medical examination revealed that the skeleton was that of a man about six feet tall and about twenty years old. But later tests by forensics experts determined that the age of the man was between eighteen and twenty-two years; Glen Hyde was twenty-nine when he disappeared. They also concluded that the victim had died no earlier than 1972. That forced speculators to look for different theories. And they did.

One of these new suppositions even involved Bessie's first husband, Earl Helmick. According to that rather far-fetched sample of reasoning, Helmick had a violent temper and was so mad at her for the divorce, he probably had something to do with her disappearance. But Helmick refused to even discuss such a scenario or become involved in any conversation that dealt with Bessie.

Although the Hydes have been gone for more than eighty years, stories about their disappearance won't die.

For several years after the incident, campers and hikers claimed they saw the Hydes living in the forests around the canyon. Then in the summer of 1971, while on a commercial river rafting expedition down the Colorado, the guide related the story of Glen and Bessie Hyde to the river runners as they sat around an evening campfire. As he presented his version of the tale, a short, elderly woman amazed her companions by declaring that she knew what had actually happened to Bessie Hyde because she *was* Bessie Hyde.

She told the campers that Glen had indeed beaten and brutalized her until she could take it no more, so she stabbed him to death. She left his body there on the floor of the Grand Canyon, hiked out to the South Rim, and started a new life as Elizabeth Cutler, away from everything she had ever known, including her own family. And with no regrets for her action.

Some believed her. The tour guide spread the word to his coworkers and they, in turn, informed all their clients that the mystery had been solved. But others weren't so accepting of the little old lady's story. Researchers soon discovered that she was four inches taller than Bessie, and birth records proved that she really was Elizabeth Cutler, born in Pomeroy, Ohio, in 1908, not Bessie Haley Hyde, who was born in Maryland in 1905. Cutler, who died in 1998, recanted her story almost immediately. She said she was a former psychologist who "simply enjoyed playing with people's minds."

The mystery took a new direction in 1992, shortly after the death of legendary river runner Georgia Clark. While going through her belongings, one of her business associates found a copy of Glen and Bessie's marriage license and a revolver tucked away in the back of Georgia's underwear drawer. The license was a certified copy with the original notary stamp on one corner, and it was issued to Glen R. Hyde and Bessie Haley. Despite that, researchers and biographers have found little to substantiate any theory that she and Bessie Hyde were the same person. But they did uncover the fact that her given name wasn't Georgia; it was Bessie. She was born Bessie DeRoss, in Oklahoma.

How Clark came into possession of the items remains a mystery, just like much of her own life. She was the first woman to run a boat through the Grand Canyon, the first woman outfitter, and the first woman to swim the canyon. But evidence discovered after her death raised the possibility that she had not been honest when talking about her past. And while she was well-liked and had many friends, no one was ever invited into her Las Vegas home. Although she never openly claimed to be Bessie Hyde, Richard Westwood, her biographer, noted that he wouldn't put it past the woman to leave the suspicious items behind simply to keep people guessing, adding, "She was not above creating things that made a good story."

And still the story lives on.

In 2005 a California theatrical company presented an American opera entitled *River's End*. According to the press reviews, the musical "tells the true story of Glen and Bessie Hyde, who began married life in a homemade boat going down the wild Colorado River." The presentation offers two possible conclusions about the couple's fate, as told by actors portraying river runners. Neither account solves anything, but the opera was well received. One critic observed that its use of lighting and sound "create a hellish, claustrophobic world of nature where a man can dream but the river rules."

But in the end, as in real life, the production inevitably gave the same answer to the same oft-asked question:

What happened to Glen and Bessie Hyde?

Only the river knows.

THE APACHE KID: A SHADOW IN ARIZONA'S HISTORY

The old highway leading from Globe to Casa Grande through the Pinal Mountains was treacherous, even on a good day. Rutted by the unyielding iron-bound wheels of wagons and stagecoaches that had been traversing it for years, the dirt road was filled with hairpin turns and steep slopes that forced the drivers of the horse-drawn vehicles to use extreme caution, regardless of how many times they had passed this way.

Sheriff Glenn Reynolds was among those who knew the road well, so while history might later question his fateful decision on the morning of November 2, 1889, it was the right one for the time. Realizing that the stagecoach probably couldn't navigate Kelvin Grade with a full load of passengers, and aware there was a good chance that a snowstorm was headed toward them, the lawman told the driver to stop at the foot of the incline. Then he ordered seven of the nine men inside the coach to get out and walk. It was a deadly mistake.

The nine men were prisoners, all headed for Yuma Territorial Prison. Eight of them were Apaches; the other was a Mexican. Convicted of many charges, including murder, they were chained together hand and foot, but their shackles left each one with a free arm. Sheriff Reynolds and his deputy, William "Hunkydory" Holmes, were well-armed and felt little danger as they trudged up the slope with the convicts. The other two prisoners were secure in the coach, and the driver, Eugene Middleton, was also armed. The hike would likely be a short one before everyone was back inside the stagecoach and their journey would resume, just like the several others the sheriff had conducted across this same path.

But not this time.

As soon as the stage disappeared over the crest of the hill, six of the convicts walking behind the stagecoach encircled and over-powered the two lawmen. Some of them began beating Holmes with large rocks, which may not have been necessary because Holmes had a heart condition and probably died of a heart attack when the attack began. But the escapees grabbed his rifle and shot him anyway. This left Reynolds outnumbered and trapped. He was unable to get off even a single shot before the prisoners wrestled his rifle away and turned it against him, killing him with three bullets to his chest.

Back on top of the hill, Middleton heard the shots and knew they could only mean trouble. But the nine-man entourage was hidden from his view, so he had no idea who had shot at whom, nor why. He'd know soon enough. Jesus Avott, the Mexican prisoner, came running up the hill and shouted a warning. But Avott spoke little English, so Middleton didn't understand what he was trying to tell him. Then he turned to look back and saw the Apaches loose, armed, and heading toward him. Seconds later, a bullet tore through his cheek and out his neck. Realizing his own life was in danger, Avott ran away into the brush rather than face the now-armed band of desperadoes.

Reynolds and Holmes were already lying lifeless on the trail, and their killers were racing toward the stagecoach. Seriously wounded and partially paralyzed, Middleton had only one chance. He fell to the ground and played dead. The convicts had removed the keys to their shackles from the bodies of the two slain lawmen. They freed themselves then unchained the two prisoners who had remained in the coach.

One of them was Na-diez-az, a convicted murderer. He would come to an ignominious end.

The other was Haskay-bay-nay-ntayl. He was better known as the Apache Kid. He was about to become a legend.

The myth that would eventually raise the Kid to some degree of immortality began innocently about thirty years before, when a boy was born into the White Mountain Apache tribe in the wilderness near Globe. His parents named him Haskay-bay-nay-ntayl. His family was part of Capitan Chi-quito's band, a peaceful group that lived in an area still known as Aravaipa Canyon. It was a near-idyllic setting—mountain springs, running streams, wooded canyons, magnificent sandstone cliffs, and plenty of game for hunting. But the area lost its innocence in 1872 when an edict from President Ulysses S. Grant established the San Carlos Indian Reservation northeast of Globe and ordered all Apaches, regardless of tribal affiliation, to move there. And stay there.

A year later, a prospector found a large, globe-shaped boulder that weighed more than seventy pounds and was assayed as almost pure silver. The discovery brought miners, settlers, bootleggers, preachers, prostitutes, and all others commonly affiliated with the chance for huge wealth into the area, forever changing the lives of the Apaches. They were consigned to the reservation, a patch of ground described by one military historian as "a gravelly flat" where the land was dotted with "scrawny, dejected lines of scattered cottonwoods, shrunken, almost leafless." It was dry, the recorder noted, and "rain was so infrequent that it took on the semblance of a phenomenon when it came at all." Dry winds swept the plain, "denuding it of every vestige of vegetation." It was also hot, he added: "In the summer a temperature of 110 degrees in the shade was cool weather."

Brought to such a place after living his formative years in the untamed wilderness of Aravaipa Canyon, the young Apache was forced to alter his lifestyle to fit into that of those whom he deemed his captors. He made the adjustment well, hanging around Globe and the government agency in charge of the reservation and doing whatever odd jobs came his way. During that time, he underwent another major change. Unable, or unwilling, to deal with his given name of Haskay-bay-nay-ntayl, the Anglos who now controlled his life began calling him "the Apache Kid," and the name stayed with him for the remainder of his life. And yet, despite all the alterations that had been thrust upon him, the Kid was known as friendly, trustworthy, intelligent, and ambitious.

Clay Beauford recognized those traits. A former Confederate soldier who migrated west and eventually became chief of the San Carlos police force, he saw potential in the teenage boy. So he took him under his wing, taught him English, let him tag along as he policed the reservation, and made him sort of a camp mascot.

The experience would lead the Kid even farther along the path that would become his destiny. The US Army was always on the lookout for scouts, and the Kid's willingness to learn made him a suitable candidate. After he applied and was accepted, another major figure entered into his life. His name was Al Sieber.

Sieber was the army's chief of scouts. He was smart and he knew the ways of the Apache. He was born in Germany, migrating with his family to Pennsylvania and then to a farming community in Minnesota. He enlisted in the First Minnesota Volunteer Infantry and saw combat in many major battles during the Civil War. He was wounded at Gettysburg, then headed west after being mustered out at the end of the war in 1865. After arriving in Arizona, Sieber was wounded again in 1875 during a battle with the Apaches north of Phoenix. More than a decade later, he was wounded a third time, and that injury spelled disaster for the Apache Kid.

Prior to that, however, Sieber had determined that the young Apache had natural leadership qualities and would be an asset to his corps, so he hired him. For the next several years, the Kid excelled as a scout. He accompanied Gen. George Crook on at least two campaigns and, by 1882, he had been promoted to the rank of sergeant. Ironically, his promotion came shortly before the Battle of Big Dry Wash, which would be the last major confrontation between the Apaches and the army in Arizona.

While on a Mexican tour, in the town of Huasabas, he was a participant in a drunken riot that almost cost him his life. Rather than have the Kid face a firing squad, however, a local judge fined him twenty dollars and the army recalled him to San Carlos.

Life was good, then. The Kid was well liked, and his ability to function as an army scout while maintaining his position and heritage among his own people had placed him in an ideal situation. Equally important, Sieber had complete trust in him. Unfortunately for all those involved, that proved to be an error in judgment on the veteran scout's part. Although he was very familiar with the Apache ways, Sieber overlooked the fact that Apache law transcended all those imposed by the white conquerors. One of the key elements of Apache law was that a wronged person had the right to settle an issue, large or small, in a manner of his own choosing. It was, in a sense, the Apache version of the infamous "eye for an eye" tradition erroneously practiced by non-Indians over the centuries.

In 1886, the Kid's father, Togo-de-Chuz, was murdered by Gon-zizzie. The two had once been rivals pursuing the same young Apache woman. Togo-de-Chuz won her hand, and she became his wife and the Kid's mother. But Gon-zizzie never forgot, and he took his vengeance by killing his former competitor. Other Indians soon caught the murderer and executed him, but the Kid suspected that Old Rip, Gon-zizzie's brother, had played a role in his father's death. He swore vengeance against him. Tribal law dictated it. That unwritten code required a man to exact blood to avenge a father's death. The Kid asked for permission to leave the reservation and go after the suspected accomplice; the request was denied. But an opportunity arose in May 1887, when Sieber left the Kid in charge of the guardhouse at San Carlos while he and another military official were away. The Kid saw his chance, and Apache justice followed. Old Rip was dispatched with a single shot.

The Apache Kid's whereabouts are still unknown.

Sieber felt betrayed and was justifiably furious when he returned to San Carlos. He ordered the Kid and four other missing scouts to give themselves up. When they did, he confined them to the same guardhouse they were supposed to be watching. His action upset other Apaches, who believed that their law superseded his law, and a small riot broke out. Someone fired a gun; that set off a hail of bullets from several different positions. None was fired by the Kid, but during the panic that followed, he and sixteen other Apaches fled. However, irreparable damage had been done. Sieber's left ankle was shattered by one of the stray bullets, and the injury would leave him crippled for the rest of his life. It changed his attitude toward the Apache Kid. When the Kid and his band surrendered peacefully a few weeks later, Sieber was foremost among his accusers as they were brought to trial. They were charged with mutiny and desertion, found guilty, and given death sentences.

Before any of the sentences could be carried out, an unexpected ally came to their defense. A veteran of the frontier conflicts, Gen. Nelson Miles intervened on their behalf, protesting that the Apaches did not understand the serious nature of their deed because, according to Apache custom, the Kid's vengeance was justified and not important enough to merit punishment. His argument was successful; the sentences were reduced. The Kid got ten years in federal prison. After serving less than a year in the island prison, Alcatraz, however, the Apaches' cases were examined by a review board which determined the jurors at their trials were prejudiced against the Indians. The sentences were thrown out.

They returned to San Carlos, but not to a happy ending. More court decisions followed, and eventually civilian and military authorities decided to apprehend all Indians accused of federal crimes and retry them in territorial courts. By the time this ruling was handed down, Al Sieber had been hobbling around on crutches for more than a year. Although he publicly acknowledged that the Kid had not fired the gun, Sieber still held him responsible. And even though the Kid was now living peacefully on the reservation, Sieber made sure his name was on the list of criminal Indians. When his trial came up, the Kid was accused of "attempting to kill Al Sieber." This time, there was no General Miles to intercede. The sentence was seven years in the territorial prison in Yuma.

On October 30, 1889, the judgments were finalized, the sheriff was given his orders, and the legend of the Apache Kid was about to burst forth into the lore of the western frontier.

Sheriff Reynolds's first selection to accompany him on the transfer of prisoners to Casa Grande was Holmes, better known as "Hunkydory" because of a poem he had written and set to the melody of an old Irish tune. One of the lines went, "hooray for hunkydory" and he sang it so often that he was given the nickname. Holmes had been prospecting in the area for more than twenty years but never struck it rich, so he took odd jobs around Globe. One of them was serving as a deputy, even though his heart condition was fairly well known in the area. Eugene Middleton, the driver, was also the owner of the stage line. He was not too thrilled about carrying the prisoners over the rugged terrain, but he eventually agreed to make the run. He climbed aboard, whistled at his horses, and guided the stage as it left Globe in the morning hours of November 1, 1889.

The trek to Casa Grande through the Pinals was about forty miles long; when they reached Casa Grande, the prisoners would be transferred to a train and shipped to Yuma. The group arrived at Riverside, the halfway point, around sunset, and made camp for the night after making sure the prisoners were all secured.

They were back on the road before sunrise, arriving at Kelvin Grade early in the morning. Sheriff Reynolds, Deputy Holmes, and seven prisoners got off the stage to lighten the load as the horses strained to haul it up the incline. No one knows for certain if the prisoners planned the attack or if they simply recognized an opportunity. The only account available was given by Avott, the horse thief, who had escaped into the brush after the brutal attack. After the others fled, he cut one of the horses loose from the stage team and rode into Florence, where he alerted authorities and told them his version of what happened.

Middleton also survived, but was unable to give complete details about the incident because he hadn't seen most of it. The crest of the hill blocked his view. But after the criminals fled, he managed to drag himself five miles back to the Riverside Station, where he sounded the alarm that triggered the largest manhunt in the history of the Arizona Territory.

It was not only the territory's largest manhunt, it was the manhunt that made the Apache Kid the shadowy figure that gives him historical importance. And at that point, all the necessary ingredients for a legend—fact, fiction, hearsay, rumor, and speculation—were thrown into a common pot.

Ironically, an act of kindness on the Apache Kid's part played an important role in the creation of his legend. After the killers freed the Kid and the other shackled passenger, two of them approached the spot where Middleton had fallen. Although stunned, he was aware that his own life was probably going to end right there. One of the murderers aimed a rifle at the driver's head and was about to shoot when the Kid ordered him to pull the rifle away. He said the man was already dead so there was little sense wasting another bullet. Then they fled, leaving two dead bodies, a wounded man, a horse thief, and a stagecoach to whatever fate awaited them there in the Pinal Mountains.

It was the last official sighting of the Apache Kid.

In the near-pandemonium that followed, immigrants to the territory got another piece of bad news. Massai, a dangerous Apache renegade, was also running loose in the area. He had escaped from a train taking Apaches to Florida and had managed to travel the 1,500 miles back to his homeland. So now there was a growing fear that Massai and the Apache Kid would team up and create havoc among the settlers.

Whether they did or not is uncertain, but the possibility was so strong that every crime perpetuated against the whites from then on was blamed on one or both of them. They knew the territory— the mountains, canyons, all the hiding places and watering holes. This gave them a major advantage over their pursuers. They easily eluded capture, and their feats became legendary.

Meanwhile, many of the others involved in the creation of the Apache Kid's emergence as a sort of folk hero were dealt their own fates. Those who had escaped with the Kid were recaptured by military and civilian patrols within ten months. Some were killed by Indian scouts, some committed suicide while in captivity.

Al Sieber served as a scout on the San Carlos Reservation for more than thirty years, but left his position after a disagreement with the military. Later, while working on a road construction crew near Globe, he was killed by a rolling boulder. A monument was erected to his memory at the scene of the accident. It's still there, along Arizona 188 near Roosevelt Dam.

But two of the central figures survived. Jesus Avott, the horse thief, was given a pardon for bringing news of the escape to the attention of authorities. Eugene Middleton, despite his near-fatal injury, lived for another forty years until his death in Globe in 1929. His grave site is near those of Sheriff Reynolds and Deputy Holmes.

The Kid was never apprehended, and details surrounding the remainder of his life up to his eventual demise remain sketchy. But they are many and they cover decades.

Regardless of what happened to him after the escape, the Kid became a veritable nightmare for those living in the central and southeastern parts of the territory. Apache Kid sightings became common from the Tonto Basin near Globe down into the Sierra Madre Mountains of northern Mexico. Almost every murder that occurred in that wide area was attributed to him, justifiably or not. Reports of his death were equally widespread, but another massacre or kidnapping usually occurred a short time later and belied the claims.

He was, according to those who lived in the area at the time, everywhere.

Those who feared him said he returned to the San Carlos Reservation several times, primarily to steal young women for temporary mating. Or that he led small outlaw bands that rustled cattle and stole food. In early 1899, an officer of the Mexican Rurales claimed that the Kid was the head of a small settlement of well-behaved Apache renegades living in the state of Chihuahua. Authorities offered monetary rewards for his capture; no one ever claimed them. Ranchers maintained he used the San Simon Valley in Arizona and Skeleton Canyon in New Mexico as avenues for his journeys to and from Mexico. In the 1920s and early 1930s, rumors began circulating that the Kid was not only seen, but had also talked with people along the Mexican border. And that he was living a peaceful existence on a ranch in the Mexican state of Sonora.

Other versions of his exploits weren't nearly so sympathetic. Some stories had the Apache Kid deserting his own brethren and becoming a loner, despised by his own and feared by Anglo settlers. He allegedly killed the young women he kidnapped after he tired of them. He preyed on lone ranchers, cowboys, and prospectors because he was a coward, afraid to deal with more than one person at a time. He was murderous and vengeful, murdering whites in retaliation for the way he claimed the Apache scouts had been mistreated by the army.

Whether true or not, the stories elevated the Kid to a legendary status. He moved like a ghost across the desert, taking whatever he wanted, killing whomever he chose. As the stories increased, so did the fear. Every noise, every shadow, could be the Apache Kid closing in for another kill. Every tree, every large rock, could be his hiding place as he waited for another victim. The theory was that by the time you saw him, it was too late.

By 1893 the reward money was up to five thousand dollars, but the Kid remained loose. He showed up at the reservation to steal another man's wife and was identified by her children. In 1894 he had a chance meeting with another former scout, asked about Sieber and the reward, then rode off. In 1924 one of the Kid's nephews claimed that his infamous uncle was alive and living in Mexico.

And with each alleged sighting, there came another alleged death story.

One involved Ed "Wallapai" Clark, an Arizona rancher. According to Clark, the Kid and his men surrounded his ranch house but Clark slipped out of the house after dark, creeping down to his corral to see two Indians leading away his favorite horse. Clark fired twice. The next morning, he found the body of a woman, supposedly a Kid wife, and a trail of blood. Clark followed the blood trail until it disappeared, but later claimed that one of his shots had mortally wounded the intruder. "It was the Kid, all right," he later said. "He crawled away to die somewhere, I know."

Another report claimed that a posse led by Charles Anderson shot and killed the Kid near Kingston, a mining camp in New Mexico, on September 10, 1905.

Another scout, Mickey Free, once brought a piece of decomposed skin to Al Sieber as proof that the Kid was dead. Free claimed that the skin bore the mark of a faint *W*, similar to those that had been tattooed on the forehead of all San Carlos males after they were forced onto the reservation. The evidence was inconclusive. None of the known photos of the Kid show the mark, but that may have been because the blue ink used in the tattooing process did not show up well in photographs.

Arizona rancher John Slaughter also claimed he was responsible for the Kid's demise. Slaughter said he killed him in the Sierra Madres but didn't tell anyone until much later because he had crossed the Mexican border and didn't want to get into legal trouble.

A group of Mexican lawmen circulated a story that they had killed the Kid in 1899. Their claim was based on the fact that one of three Apaches they had slain was carrying Sheriff Reynolds's pistol and watch. The Mexicans assumed that the Kid would more than likely have kept these items after the massacre, so they presumed that the current owner was the Kid himself, even though there was no proof that he had actually taken the items after the escape. That version was quickly shot full of holes because the dead Apache was an old man with long white hair, and the Kid would have been in his mid-thirties at the time.

In September 1906, a New Mexican posse following a trail of stolen horses along the north rim of Wild Horse Canyon ambushed two Indians. The first was killed instantly but the second, although badly wounded, escaped into the thicket. Later that day, an Apache woman was apprehended in a nearby town. She said she was the wife of the Apache Kid and that he was the second person shot by the posse. Searchers later found a skeleton in the immediate area and assumed it was his. New Mexican authorities gave that version so much credence that they named a mountain peak after him, and designated a site on the peak as the Kid's grave site. It's in the San Mateo Mountains of the Cibola National Forest. The supposed grave site is one mile northwest of Apache Kid Peak, in Cyclone Saddle.

But that story has also been told with a different ending. In this one, the woman said she was married to Massai, and it was his remains the searchers found.

Since none of the claims was supported by actual fact, the question of what actually happened to the Apache Kid, and when it actually happened, remains a mystery. The most common theory is that he lived his final years in peace before succumbing to old age in Mexico.

But his legend is forever emblazoned into the history of the Old West and is still remembered in a variety of ways.

Historians and researchers are still debating his actual name. The consensus is that it was Haskay-bay-nay-ntayl, but some claim it was Hashkee-binaa-nteel while others claim it was Ski-be-nan-ted.

In 1980 the Congress of the United States designated 44,626 acres in the San Mateo Mountains of western New Mexico as the Apache Kid Wilderness. The area contains a sixty-eight-mile trail system; the main trail leads to the spot where that posse allegedly gunned him down in 1906, and to the marker proclaiming it as the Kid's grave site.

Author Phyllis de la Garza has written a well-researched biography entitled *The Apache Kid*. Dan Thrapp deals with the Kid's relationship with his army-scout mentor in his book, *Al Sieber, Chief of Scouts*. And the Apache Kid was a fictional Old West character in the Marvel Comics universe of superheroes back in the 1950s. The comic book character was named after the real Apache Kid but was totally unrelated to him.

A professional wrestler who grew up on the San Carlos Reservation performed on the pro circuit for several years as "the Apache Kid," but outside of the fact that both he and the real Kid were Apaches, there was no connection.

In 1930 cowboy hero Jack Perrin starred in *Apache Kid's Escape*, a two-fisted sagebrusher movie filled with shootouts, horseback chases, and other Old West action. In 1941 Donald "Red" Barry was the hero in a B Western entitled *The Apache Kid*. Neither bore any resemblance to the real legend.

GABRIELLE DARLEY: HEARTLESS MURDERESS OR INNOCENT VICTIM?

The price of admission into the Elks Movie Theater that night in 1928 was a dime, well within Gabrielle Melvin's reach. She was, after all, one of the wealthiest women in Prescott. She wore diamonds and a fancy dress as she walked past the boys handing out flyers that billed the evening's presentation as "a startling exposé of the white slave trade." She bought a ticket, strode past the mannequin in the lobby wearing a garish red robe, and followed an usher to a seat. Then she sat back to enjoy *The Red Kimona*, the feature film.

The organist, a standard fixture in movie halls, kept the crowd entertained until the theater darkened and the curtains drew back to reveal the giant screen, black at first then gradually illuminated. The standard requests for good behavior flashed across the reflective surface. In a silent movie, the organist's task was to set the mood. His music swelled and softened accordingly as the action began. In the opening scene, a woman leafed through a collection of old newspapers. She stopped at one and began reading a particular article. The camera panned in to scan the headline. It blared: "Story of Gabrielle Darley: Startling Human Document." The

Gabrielle Darley-Wiley's life was filled with mysterious deaths.

woman turned to the audience and, through the use of gestures, exaggerated facial expressions, and subtitles at the bottom of the screen, revealed that this was a true story. One of the subtitles said, "If it contains bitter truths, remember that I only turn the pages of the past."

Out in the audience, Gabrielle Melvin sat shocked.

As the movie continued, her shock turned to anger, then outrage. She was Gabrielle Darley. She was seeing herself being portrayed on the screen. Nobody told her beforehand that her life story had been made into a movie. Even worse, a lot of it was true, and the true parts were the worst parts. She didn't like it, and she planned to take action.

She did, and several lives were changed as a result, most notably hers and that of Dorothy Davenport Reid, the producer of the movie and also the actress appearing in the uncredited role of the woman poring over the old newspapers.

Although Gabrielle Darley's life actually was a prime subject for such a movie, this one contained a major mistake. Reid, the producer, should have followed the common moviemaking practice and changed Darley's name. She made the alteration for every other real person depicted, but not the lead character. She never explained her reasoning, not even during the five years of court battles that ensued. Presumably, however, she did it to create some publicity for the film and entice people who remembered the trial into the theaters.

In the movie, Darley was played by Priscilla Bonner, at that time a fairly well-known actress who also appeared in such other silents as *Long Pants, It, Three Bad Men, Earth Woman, Proud*

Flesh, and *Charley's Aunt*. The film was also the directorial debut of Walter Lang, who later helmed such talkies as *Tin Pan Alley*, *State Fair*, *Mother Wore Tights*, *Cheaper by the Dozen*, *Call Me Madam*, *The King and I*, and *There's No Business Like Show Business*. His final film, made in 1961, was the less-than-classic *Snow White and the Three Stooges*. Despite that, he earned a star on the Hollywood Walk of Fame.

The film opened in 1925, and while the original title, *The Red Kimono*, was spelled correctly, after repeated misspellings its producers surrendered and let it become *The Red Kimona*. The plot depicts Darley as a prostitute in New Orleans. Flashbacks later reveal that she grew up under the heel of an evil father and a mother who didn't care. To escape that miserable lifestyle, she takes up with one Howard Blaine, falls in love, and expects to live happily after. But Blaine instead gives her a red kimono, sets her up in her own apartment in the red-light district, and turns her into a call girl. According to the movie, she agrees to the sordid life because she is in love with Blaine.

But Blaine deserts her, takes all her earnings, and runs off to Los Angeles to marry someone else. Darley follows him, confronts him in a jewelry store, and shoots him. She is arrested and tried for murder. A jury believes her story about all the mistreatment she has undergone and she is acquitted.

A socialite takes her in, but with ulterior motives. Because Darley is somewhat of a celebrity, the woman drags her along to tea parties and high-society events and displays her as sort of a pet, but soon tires of her and kicks her out. Left to fend for herself, Darley can't hold a job once her employers find out about her past.

A return to her earlier occupation appears to be her only hope. But does she go back? No, because true love finally comes along in the form of a chauffeur. The film ends with Reid making another appearance to deliver an impassioned plea to give fallen women a second chance.

The film was not well received. One critic said it had "some nice direction but ultimately there wasn't a lot to separate it from other melodramas of the period." An entertainment critic for the *New York Times* wasn't nearly so kind. He wrote, "There have been a number of wretched pictures on Broadway during the last year, but none seemed to have quite reached the low level of 'The Red Kimona,' a production evidently intended to cause weeping, wailing and gnashing of teeth. Possibly it might accomplish its purpose if the theater doors were locked, but so long as one can get out of the building, it is another matter."

Another reviewer noted, "The movie is an unbearable tear-jerker . . . unconvincing and too banal to strike a chord for those caught in such dire circumstances. . . . This film is worth a look only for historical reasons and to see how melodrama was done before there were talkies."

Had she merely been accused of producing a bad movie, Dorothy Reid's troubles might have ended there. She was well established in Hollywood. Her father, Harry Davenport, was a familiar Hollywood character actor, and she made her own stage and movie debuts when she was only sixteen. In 1912 she appeared in *His Only Son*, a Western. Her costar was Wallace Reid, and the two formed a moviemaking partnership, then married. Their relationship ended tragically when Wallace was injured in a train wreck on location and eventually died of morphine addiction at age thirty-one. He left his widow with two children, financial security, and a mansion on Sunset Boulevard. She became an antidrug crusader and produced and starred in *Human Wreckage*, a drama dedicated to her late husband and his addiction. One newspaper review called it "the most important picture ever made." She then produced *The Red Kimona* about two years later.

But none of that quelled Gabrielle's fury, and shortly after seeing the movie, she filed a fifty-thousand-dollar lawsuit against Reid for invasion of privacy. In court she noted that although she actually did shoot and kill a former lover, she was speedily acquitted by a Los Angeles jury. Afterwards, she said, she settled down in Prescott, Arizona, married, and became a respectable member of the town's society.

She claimed that none of her friends and neighbors knew about her past, but when the movie was released using her real name, she found herself ostracized. She further testified that the movie depicted her as a "woman of lewd character, a prostitute and a murderer." Although those inferences were basically true, an appellate court upheld her suit and expressed outrage over Reid's error in judgment. The court's ruling said, "It was wrong to destroy Gabrielle's reputation, wrong to injure her standing in society by publishing the story of her former depravity for the sole purpose of making money." Reid appealed to the California Supreme Court, but that body refused to hear the case.

At that point, truth and fiction wander off on completely divergent paths.

The real Gabrielle Darley was born in France in 1890. She would later claim that her father was abusive, so her mother left him, took their daughter, and moved to San Francisco, where she was killed in the 1906 earthquake. Left without parents at age fifteen, Gabrielle moved to the Nevada gold fields, where she tried to eke out a living by waiting tables. But that life was too hard and hardly profitable. At the age of sixteen, she turned to prostitution, but she did it all by herself, not with the help of a scoundrel as the movie suggested. Young, pretty, and worldly, she did well in the profession. She invested much of her earnings in diamonds and planned to open her own brothel with what was left over.

In 1909 she married Ernest Presti, an Italian-born gambler and boxer who used the name Kid Kirby in the ring. The couple moved to Prescott, where both plied their respective trades. Gabrielle was very successful. Although only nineteen, she opened her own house of ill repute and ran it as a highly profitable operation. But her husband was neither a good gambler nor a skilled pugilist. And because he was such a consistent loser in both ventures, he started depleting his wife's savings at an alarming rate.

That ended one day in May of 1911 when Presti was shot and killed by a shoeshine man over a twenty-dollar gambling debt. The incident cast some suspicion upon Gabrielle. In view of the fact that Presti was dipping into her finances, some suggested she had a good reason to have him killed. She was never formally accused, but the shooting set the tone for the rest of her life. It also should have served as a warning for other men she encountered, because she married four times and each husband met with a less-than-satisfactory end.

The next man in her life was Leonard Topp, the person depicted as "Howard Blaine" in the movie. Their relationship is sketchy, but he apparently frequented Gabrielle's place of business on a regular basis and eventually became her lover. That didn't end well either. Topp ran off with one of Gabrielle's working girls after absconding with a fortune in the madam's diamonds, as well as a substantial amount of cash. It was a fatal mistake on his part. His ex-mistress hired a private detective to track them down; he found them in Los Angeles, and Gabrielle followed. One account says she encountered him in a jewelry store where he was allegedly buying a diamond ring for his new girlfriend. Another says they had their final meeting in a liquor store that Topp had purchased with the money he had stolen from her. Either way, the end result was the same.

Dressed in her finest attire, Gabrielle walked into the store and hissed, "Hello, Leonard." According to eyewitness accounts, just as Topp spun around to face her, she fired the pistol she had concealed in her fur muff. Her aim was deadly. The bullet hit Topp's heart, but he lived long enough to knock her down and smash her head against the floor. After knocking her unconscious, Topp got up and said, "Well, I guess I'm about through for good," then fell over dead. Gabrielle was arrested and charged with murder.

The trial was a sensation all across the country. Headlines screamed, "She Did It Because She Loved Him!" One of her sporting girls testified that Topp was an abuser whose favorite pastime was kicking Gabrielle while wearing his heavy boots. The coverage of the trial frequently knocked World War I stories off the front pages. In some of the reports, Gabrielle was likened to Frankie, who was done wrong by her man in the popular ballad "Frankie and Johnny." Appearing contrite and wearing the countenance of a woman who had been victimized, she gave the jury her best impression of a lost soul adrift in a heartless world. An outraged, all-male jury deliberated for less than eight minutes before returning a verdict of not guilty. Adela Rogers St. John, a newspaper reporter who covered the trial, commented that with men like Topp, "homicide is not only justifiable, but obligatory."

Gabrielle brought up all that in her lawsuit, which received almost equal coverage. The country had never seen or heard anything like this before. The case drew so much attention that even the *New York Times* gave it regular coverage. In a sense the entire movie industry was on trial for using actual facts when filming a biographical movie. It was all because a prostitute not only stood up to Hollywood and waged a five-year legal war against the moguls, but she also won the case. Although terms of the settlement were never disclosed, Reid did lose her mansion and a large sum of money. But it didn't ruin her. Although forced into bankruptcy by the verdict, she continued her crusade against drugs, returned to Hollywood, and worked as a writer until her death in 1977. One of her final efforts came in the 1950s when she cowrote the scripts for the *Francis the Talking Mule* movie series.

Adela Rogers St. John made out all right, however. After the actual murder trial, she interviewed Gabrielle and wrote an account of her life for the *San Francisco Examiner* in 1918. Although filled with fabrications, half-truths, and products of Gabrielle's vivid imagination, the article was considered such a shocking exposé that it drew readers by the thousands. Rogers St. John later used the story when she penned the screenplay for *The Red Kimona*.

Unlike the ending of the movie, the real Gabrielle did not give up her life of sin once the trial was over. Instead, she returned to Prescott and resumed her role as a madam, operating out of several downtown hotels along the city's infamous Whiskey Row. Making rare appearances during the daylight hours, she was accepted but not respected by the other residents of Prescott. And when she did stroll down the streets, she flashed her diamonds in arrogant displays of her ill-gotten wealth. Her fellow Prescottonians said she was pretty but plump, dressed in a businesslike manner, and dyed her hair frequently. They also said she took good care of "her girls," even sending some of them to business school so they could find employment once their days as call girls were over.

She also took another husband.

This time the unfortunate spouse was Bernard Melvin. They met in California, married in Orange County, and divided their time between Prescott and California. Six months later, they split up, and the cause was a familiar scenario. Just like her two previous mates, Melvin got sticky fingers and dug into Gabrielle's bank accounts. She went to California, had him arrested, and charged him with embezzling two thousand dollars from her. The Los Angeles newshounds, aware that Gabrielle Darley was back in the area, jumped all over the story. She refused their requests for interviews, but Melvin was more than willing. "I didn't steal that money from her," he told the *Los Angeles Times* from his jail cell. "She gave it to me. We loved each other once, but we're through now and she hates me. She hated Topp and she killed him. I'm in jail. The man pays, I guess."

Melvin was convicted and served time. He then returned to Prescott and lived in a shack at the town dump ground, where he worked as a caretaker. In 1927 he was beaten and robbed, and once again, there was some suspicion aimed at his former wife. But she was never formally charged. Melvin, a pathetic loner who avoided all contact with the outside world, died in 1929 as a result of the injuries suffered during the robbery. He was seventy.

Three men in her life; three deaths.

But Gabrielle wasn't done taking strolls down the bridal path. Shortly after Melvin's demise, she took the vows with Everett Fretz, a local barber and manicurist. It was another short-lived union. Fretz began having mental problems. He raved about an imaginary gold mine near Prescott and said people were out to steal it from him. He demanded that the sheriff deputize him so he could protect it. The rantings became so bad that he was committed to the Arizona State Asylum in 1935. He died a short time after the commitment. Although his symptoms were similar to those caused by ingesting poison, state records said it was the result of "general paralysis of the insane." He was forty years old.

But Gabrielle Presti Melvin Fretz still wasn't done looking for love.

It came this time in the form of George Wiley. By now Gabrielle was past her prime. She was an aging hooker, plump and frowsy, but always decked out in her beloved diamonds. Her intended was a short, overweight, red-faced former bootlegger. They were married on July 31, 1937, and left Prescott to operate the combination liquor store, cafe, auto court, and gas station they had purchased in nearby Salome. Gabrielle began using her nickname of Dollie, and life went on as before. Despite the change in locale, she still had her "her girls." But now she ran them out of the cabins behind the cafe instead of the fashionable hotels of Prescott. And then, almost as if fulfilling some grand design, death found her again.

In late 1940, Wiley and Mae Grisson, one of Dollie's working girls, got into an argument at the cafe. The angry words soon led to a physical confrontation. Wiley lunged at the girl, and she fell backwards off her stool and hit her head on a water cooler. She was taken to a hospital in Wickenburg, where she died two weeks later, shortly after Dollie had paid her a visit. George Wiley was charged with murder, and his trial was scheduled for early 1941. It never happened.

On January 10, 1941, the accused man was found dead in his home. After working the midnight shift at the cafe, Wiley went home, where he drank from a glass his wife allegedly had left out for him. The glass contained rat poison. When she returned home, Dollie discovered his lifeless body sprawled out on the kitchen floor. The rumors started almost immediately. It was an understandable reaction due to the numbers involved: Four husbands, one live-in lover, five deaths under unusual circumstances.

A coroner's inquest was called because there were suggestions that Dollie had purposely left the tainted glass out for him. There were also hints that maybe Mae Grisson, her husband's purported victim, hadn't died from her head injury but as a result of poison. The coroner's jury ignored such speculation and ruled that the girl had died of natural causes, and that Wiley's death was a suicide.

Now very well-off financially, Gabrielle literally abandoned her given name and became known as Dollie Wiley. She also gave up her life as a madam. Some said it was because she regretted ever becoming involved with the profession; others snorted and said it was because Yavapai County officials were cracking down on prostitution. Regardless of the reason, she quit the girls-for-hire business and spent most of her time operating the multipurpose facility in Salome. But death came knocking once more, in mid-August of 1962.

Bill Gabbard, who ran a service station in Salome and rented a house from Dollie, shot and killed a man while hunting. Now it was Gabrielle's turn to rise to someone else's defense. She helped Gabbard's wife hire a top lawyer and posted his bail. The jury delivered a verdict of not guilty. Dollie Wiley wept when she heard it. In a sense, she knew what he had gone through because there were eerie similarities to his case and the ordeal she had undergone in 1915—a fatal gunshot, a plea of self-defense, acquittal, and a second chance.

Ironically, the possibility of a second chance was the supposed theme of *The Red Kimona*. At the end of the movie, Reid made another brief appearance and pleaded that fallen women should be given a chance for redemption. It was not the only strange twist in the complex story. At her murder trial, Gabrielle was defended by Earl Rogers, a leading Los Angeles criminal attorney. He was Adela Rogers St. John's father.

All that became irrelevant when death made its final appearance in the saga of Gabrielle Darley. Five days after helping Gabbard escape a wrongful jail sentence, she fell and broke her hip.

She was taken to a hospital in Wickenburg, where she developed pneumonia. Realizing that the end was near, she contacted friends in Prescott, who brought a preacher to administer last rites. She died on Christmas Day 1962, at age seventy-two. Her body was cremated and the ashes interred next to the grave of Everett Fretz, one of the soul mates who had preceded her in death.

ARIZONA'S LOST TREASURES: THEY'RE STILL WAITING

Deep within the heart of anyone who lives in Arizona, or anyone who has ever been to Arizona, or anyone who plans to come to Arizona, there is this one common fear:

Somebody's going to find the Lost Dutchman Mine before I can get to it.

Whoever does uncover the mine, or any of the other treasures supposedly hidden in the state's sands and mountains, will be rich. Not as rich as winning the lottery, perhaps, but rich nonetheless.

Much of the lore surrounding the buried gold centers around the Lost Dutchman Mine, hidden for more than a century in the mysterious Superstition Mountains. To the geologist, the Superstitions are a single mountain composed of tuff, contoured by the elements into peaks and canyons. To the writer, they are brooding land masses, relentless wilderness and foreboding rock sculptures that loom against a jagged horizon. The dreamer envisions them as last strongholds of solitude still safe from the encroachments of civilization. And the detective wonders why so many people go there and never come back.

But the treasure hunter does not dwell upon such intangibles. He goes to the Superstitions for one reason—to find gold.

Arizona has more stories of lost treasure than any other state, and any discussion of the subject inevitably leads to the intertwined and unresolved mystery involving the Superstitions, the Lost Dutchman Mine, and Jacob Waltz.

History records that there is gold in the Superstitions. However, it does not record where it is. So the treasure-seekers rely on old maps, aged ramblings, hearsay, and speculation in their quest for untold wealth.

The basis for the story of the Lost Dutchman Mine goes back to a time when only Apache Indians lived in and around the area east of what would become Phoenix. They probably found the gold but had no use for it. Then the Spanish conquistadors arrived, looking for the legendary Seven Cities of Cibola, a place where the streets were paved with gold and the women wore solid gold armbands. The natives warned the interlopers against looking for the gold, saying it was guarded by their Thunder God. The Spaniards ignored them, but ultimately fled when their men began disappearing.

Both the gold and the land were left untouched until around 1845, when don Miguel Peralta, a wealthy Mexican landowner, discovered a vein of rich gold ore. He made mental notes and maps, went back to Mexico for men and supplies, then returned to begin a mining operation. It produced fabulous wealth, which he then shipped back to Mexico. His presence did not sit well with the Apaches.

Three years after Peralta's initial incursion, the natives mobilized a large group of warriors to drive the treasure hunters from their lands. Peralta somehow heard about their plans and ordered his men to pack up and leave, but not before they took elaborate steps to conceal the mine. It was a costly mistake, because it delayed their departure. The Apaches attacked and massacred the entire group, then drove their heavily burdened pack animals off cliffs and into ravines. Later prospectors would find the animals' remains, still carrying sacks of gold. The last discovery of that nature occurred in 1914 when a prospector showed up in Phoenix with the well-rotted remains of a Spanish saddle, some decayed leather straps, and about eighteen thousand dollars in gold ore.

Although tales of the Peralta mine were numerous, nobody reported seeing it until 1870. That year a group of Apaches approached Dr. Abraham Thorne, an army doctor who had been living with the Indians and was considered a friend. As a reward for his kindness toward them, they offered to take him to a gold mine, but only if he agreed to go there blindfolded. When the group arrived at the bottom of a canyon, the Apaches removed the blindfold, showed the doctor a stack of gold nuggets, and told him to take as many as he could carry. Once back at his post, Dr. Thorne sold the nuggets for about six thousand dollars.

Next came the Dutchman.

Jacob Waltz (sometimes spelled Walz) wasn't really Dutch. He came from Germany, but "Dutch" was easier to pronounce than "Deutschland," so he became "the Dutchman." He arrived in the United States in 1845 and spent the next twenty years prospecting in the East, Midwest, and Southwest. In 1870 he took a steady job at the Vulture Mine near Wickenburg, where he met Jacob Weiser. They formed a loose relationship and struck out for the Superstitions. Waltz had heard the stories about the lost Peralta mine, guarded by a supernatural entity. From that point on, the story of the Lost Dutchman Mine becomes a mixture of fact, fiction, folklore, and suggestion, blended with deception, accusations, and speculation.

According to some theories, the two miners saved a Mexican man's life and he repaid them by giving them a map that allegedly showed the location of the Peralta mine. That version maintains that the Mexican was don Miguel Peralta, and that Waltz and Weiser not only found the mine, but eventually bought it from Peralta. Other stories suggest they either stumbled on the mine by accident or killed two Mexican miners and took their gold.

Regardless of how they got it, the two became known as big spenders in the Phoenix area for several years, until Weiser mysteriously disappeared. Waltz never had an explanation for the disappearance, leading to speculation that he had killed his partner in a dispute over the mine. Another version says Weiser wandered off into the wilderness and was killed by Apaches. Despite the inferences, Waltz hung around Phoenix, frequently buying drinks in local saloons and paying for them with gold nuggets. When the gold ran out, he went back into the mountains and got more. If asked about the location of the mine, he gave conflicting directions; when others tried to trail him into the wilderness, he easily eluded them.

But time ran out long before the gold did. In 1891, sick and bedridden, the old Dutchman died in the home of Julia Thomas, his caretaker. He had promised to take Thomas to his mine when he was feeling better, but the time never came. He died on October 15, a sack of gold stashed beneath his bed. Shortly afterward,

Thomas launched a series of expeditions into the Superstitions, convinced that Waltz had given her enough information about the mine site that she could find it. She never did. Neither have the hundreds who have followed secondhand reports and secret maps into the Superstitions.

And while he's been dead for more than a century, Jacob Waltz is still a good source of revenue for many. His mine has become a cottage industry. A wide variety of books purport to describe the exact location. Several prospectors claim they've found the mine but need grubstake money to work it. Those gullible enough to invest have yet to see any returns. Almost every souvenir shop in the Phoenix area hawks treasure maps that supposedly reveal precisely which shadow of which peak points to the mine at a certain time of the day.

Movie buffs who need more information might seek out a copy of *Lust for Gold*, a 1949 Columbia Pictures production that starred Glenn Ford as the Dutchman and Ida Lupino as his love interest.

About the only constant in all the stories is that the mine is located somewhere near Weaver's Needle, a towering lava plug. Don Peralta had earlier called it Sombrero Peak; others dubbed it the Finger of God. The current name comes from Paulino Weaver, an early explorer who carved his name into the rock. Subsequent treasure hunters saw his name and applied it to the landmark.

The search goes on. It is always futile; it is frequently deadly.

Since 1870, when stories about the lost mine first began circulating, about forty people have either disappeared or been found dead in and around the suspected location of the Lost Dutchman

Mine. Guy "Hematite" Frank, who returned from the mountain in 1937 with a number of rich gold samples, was among them. He was found shot to death on the side of a trail. Next to his body was a small sack of gold ore. In 1947 prospector James Cravey used a helicopter to search for the mine. The pilot set him down near Weaver's Needle, but Cravey failed to hike out as planned. A search discovered his camp but not the prospector. His headless skeleton was found in a canyon months later. In 1960, while attempting to drill a hole through Weaver's Needle, engineer Robert St. Marie was shot and killed by Edward Piper, a prospector. Two months later, Piper was found dead, allegedly of a perforated ulcer.

The last recorded Lost Mine–related death occurred in 1984 when the body of prospector Walt Gasler was found near the alleged site. He had spent much of his life searching for the mine. In his pack, authorities discovered gold that had the same characteristics as the rich ore Jacob Waltz had found earlier.

Fortune hunters who despair at ever finding the Dutchman's lode should not give up hope, however. Plenty of other opportunities exist within Arizona's borders, because there's lost gold all over the state. Finding it is the problem. For starters, some members of the Tohono O'odham tribe of southeastern Arizona believe that the Baboquivera Mountain Range, which they hold sacred, is filled with gold and that all the gold in the state has filtered down from there. Their traditions say that I'itoi, the god who created them, lives in a cave on the mountain and sometimes comes down to give the people advice. Many years ago, according to their legend, some Spanish explorers were digging for gold on the mountain and it opened up and swallowed them.

Other hidden caches aren't so carefully guarded, but they're just as hard to access. Up near Lake Powell, tales still circulate about the treasure buried by John D. Lee, a Mormon who assisted in the slaughter of 122 pioneers in Utah's 1857 Mountain Meadows Massacre. Lee was eventually prosecuted, convicted, and executed by the church's leaders. Before being captured and tried, however, he fled the Mormon compound and went into hiding in one of the many canyons that abound along the Arizona-Utah border. According to a letter he wrote to one of his nineteen wives, Lee hid his life savings in the canyon and sent her a map showing the location.

Typically, reports of how much he buried and where he buried it vary, depending upon who is telling the story. Some reports say his life savings included seven cans of pure gold; others swear it was gold coins worth one hundred thousand dollars, stolen from the settlers he helped murder. Since all firsthand accounts have vanished, it's probable that Lee did hide some treasure somewhere, but he hid it so well that no will ever find it.

In the center of the state, on a hilltop near Winkleman, a spiral-shaped hole conceals the Golden Chimney of the Aravaipas, a secret worth millions. In this scenario, the bones of Thomas F. McLean are considered major clues to the existence of a hidden treasure. McLean came out West after being court-martialed by the US Military Academy for numerous violations. Bitter over the expulsion, McLean renounced his white heritage and took up with the Aravaipa Apaches. He married one, began dressing in breech-clouts and moccasins, and took the name "Yuma." He also observed that the Indians often settled their debts with gold nuggets or free gold from quartz. This got his attention and, according to several accounts, made him a wealthy man. But only for a short time.

One story says he befriended an Aravaipa chief and duped him into revealing where his people were finding all those nuggets. The chief agreed, but on the condition that Yuma could make only one trip to the site and could never reveal what he saw. If he did, the chief warned, bad things would happen to both of them. The two rode into the mountains near Camp Grant and stopped at an eight-foot depression. Yuma took out his knife and began scraping, and he found the top of a chimneylike formation that contained free gold so thick that the blade of his knife couldn't fit between the chunks. He was allowed to take as much as he could carry, which should have been enough to provide him with a comfortable lifestyle. Another version says Yuma often went on mysterious trips with several Apaches, and each time he returned loaded down with gold.

But his story did not end well. Yuma allegedly hooked up with another Anglo and led him to the secret chimney, where they dug up about thirty pounds of quartz. They packed the ore back to Tucson, where it assayed at more than fifty thousand dollars in gold per ton. The local newspaper, the *Arizona Daily Citizen*, got hold of the story and wrote that "there was enough for all, and great fortunes were anticipated by those who were to participate in the new El Dorado." Yuma, worried that the Apaches would find out he had broken his promise never to return to the site, hid out until the furor died down. It wasn't long enough. A few months later, while traveling with his wife in the desert, they were attacked by vengeful Apaches and clubbed to death. His accomplice in the ill-fated adventure didn't fare any better. He went back to Camp Grant, intent on digging up more gold, but was warned against it by the camp commander. He ignored the advice. A few days later, soldiers found his horse and an empty revolver, but no sign of the man.

Another fortune lies buried—in the strictly literal sense—at Sunset Crossing on the Little Colorado River. In 1865, a prospector who had struck it rich in the gold fields of California was returning home to Illinois, accompanied by his wife. The man had hit pay dirt. He was carrying a bonanza of about three hundred thousand dollars in gold dust when they arrived at the crossing. But his wife became ill and died in a matter of days. Saddened by the man's loss, the owner of the trading post agreed to build a wooden box for a coffin and clear some land for a grave site. At the hastily arranged funeral, the woman's coffin was so surprisingly heavy that it took six men to place it in the grave. No one thought much about it at the time, and the prospector returned to Illinois. Years later he revealed that he had placed half his gold, an estimated $150,000 worth, in the coffin as his wife's share. This brought a flurry of activity, but no one has ever found the coffin and the gold it allegedly contains.

The Case of the Bumbling Bandits affords the determined gold seeker with another venue. It happened in 1895 when a Southern Pacific train was held up by a pair of inept, or at least explosive-challenged, bandits. The robbers forced the rail crew to unhook the mail car carrying a large amount of money, then ordered the remainder of the cars, along with the engine, to continue on to their destination. Once they had the mail car to themselves, the pair tried to dynamite the safe. In order to hold it steady, they placed a bunch of sacks on top of the safe while they experimented with the proper amount of dynamite required to blow the door open. Unfortunately for the bandits, they used too much blasting powder. The explosion not only tore the door off the safe, but also destroyed the sacks they were using for ballast.

Then they discovered that there was very little money inside the safe, but the sacks that they had just blown into the atmosphere contained gold coins. The bandits were captured and a majority of the coins were recovered. But modern legend says there are still about one thousand of them scattered across the desert in the Dos Cabeza Mountains five miles southeast of Willcox.

Geronimo, the fabled Apache leader, also plays a role in the ongoing search for lost gold. According to some, while imprisoned at Fort Sill, Oklahoma, Geronimo tried to bribe any army officer by promising to reveal the location of a rich gold mine in exchange for his release. That story says Geronimo and his Apache followers discovered a rich gold vein in Sycamore Canyon near the mouth of the Verde River in the Clarkdale area. But Spanish soldiers seized the mother lode, constructed a smelter, and soon had a multitude of gold bars tucked away in a cave.

The Apaches tried to scare the soldiers away by rolling boulders down on them from atop the canyon wall, but the tactic didn't work, and soon the invaders had so much gold, they decided to transport some of it to Mexico on mules. They never got there. As they hiked out of the canyon, the Apaches ambushed the mining party, intent on killing all of them. But two soldiers escaped and hid out during the attack. When the Apaches left, the soldiers returned to their camp and stored the remaining gold bars in the mine tunnel, then sealed the entrance. The pair then made their

Weaver's Needle shimmers in the Superstition Mountains, marking the possible site of lost gold.

way to Tubac. They told their story to prospectors who immediately headed for the site to search for the treasure. They found only the ruins of a building but not the gold bars.

Years later, a group of miners found the mine but, like those who came before them, not the gold bars. They worked the mine for a while and did retrieve some gold ore before coming under attack by Apaches. The Indians routed the Anglos then destroyed all traces of the mine site. Only a few miners escaped; none was brave enough to go back to relocate the treasure.

In the first half of the nineteenth century, a prospector came across traces of an old mine operating near Tumacácori, an abandoned mission near Tubac. This was all the proof the fortune hunters needed. According to the legends already circulating among their kind, the mission had served not as a place of worship but as a mill and smelter for a gold-mining operation.

In one scenario the Jesuit missionaries who were operating the mission—and, allegedly, the mine—learned they were being exiled back to Spain by an edict of the king, so they loaded nearly three thousand burros with silver and gold, carried the treasure to the mine, and buried the entrance. They planned to come back for it but were never allowed to leave Spain again. An estimated twenty-five million dollars in gold and silver may now lie hidden under sacred ground.

A second version of that tale comes to an even more intriguing finale. In it the friars found a rich silver mine near the mission and forced the local Opata Indians to work it for them. After the ore was smelted, the bars were stacked in a giant room at the back of the mine. The Opatas also used the room for their own religious rites, a combination of the missionaries' preachings and their own paganism. They captured a young Indian woman because they thought she was the Blessed Virgin Mary and ordered her to mate with their chief to produce a child savior. When she refused, her captors threatened to sacrifice her to their gods. They tied her to the pile of silver, gave her one last chance to change her mind, then murdered her and went into their ritual dances.

When the missionaries heard the commotion, they rushed to the mine and found the young woman's body. Infuriated and appalled that their teachings had produced such a deadly result, the holy men drove the Indians away then sealed the mine entrance. According to the legend, the silver and the skeletal remains of the woman still lie beneath the ground near the mission, waiting to be found. But they probably never will be because the mission and the surrounding area are now a national monument.

Missionaries also play a major role in still another legend of the lost gold. This story tells about the fate of a Spanish mission on Tohono O'odham land north of the Arizona-Mexico border. The natives helped built a church and an orderly little village surrounding it, which the priests named Mission San Marcelo de Sonoita. When they finished that project, the Indians were ordered to work a gold mine in the San Francisco Mountains to the south, across the Mexican border. They also built a smelter and fashioned the gold into bars which were stored, along with bags filled with nuggets and dust, in a secret room under the mission. But according to the legend, the natives grew tired of being overworked and rebelled one Sunday in 1750. A group of warriors walked into the morning service with blankets thrown over their upper bodies, as was their custom. When they filled the church, the men pulled out weapons from beneath the blankets and killed the resident priest and two visiting clergymen.

The attackers threw the bodies into the underground chamber where the treasure was hidden then leveled the church down to its very foundations, burying the bodies and the gold. They also covered the entrance to the rich gold mine where they had been subjected to forced labor. The whereabouts of both, if they ever existed, remain a mystery.

There are several versions of that tale. One indicates that the Indians working with the priests were loyal to them and did not feel enslaved. They cared for the priests and, when they heard of plans for the attack, they warned the holy men and helped them hide the gold in a cave in the nearby Tortilla Mountains before leading them to safety. Other accounts say the gold now lies in a cavern in the Puerto Blanco Mountains in Pima County.

Bumble Bee, located about forty-five miles north of Phoenix, never was much of a town, and today there's little there except a few private homes and the remains of what was supposed to be a touristy "ghost town." However, if one legend bears any truth, there's about eighty thousand dollars' worth of gold buried in Bronco Canyon, about four miles east of Bumble Bee. It got there in the mid-1800s when two prospectors struck it rich. Because they didn't have the equipment to smelt the rich ore they found, they hid it under a large rock near their camp. It would be safe there, the two assumed, while they went back to their homes over the winter. Things didn't go as they planned, however. Before they could leave their camp, an Apache war party attacked and killed one of them. The other man escaped but was so frightened by the incident that he refused to go back to the camp until the Indian wars were over.

But the surviving miner was an old man by that time, and died before he could return to the mine. On his deathbed he told his story to friends and relatives and even tried to describe the location, but those who searched for the place never found it. Several have found traces of a mine; none has found any gold.

While most of the legends deal with burning sands, hidden canyons, and mountain peaks, one that still circulates in the Flagstaff area involves a watery grave.

During the winter of 1891, two outlaws hatched a get-rich-quick scheme that might have worked if they hadn't encountered frigid weather and a determined sheriff. The pair stole eight large

SAM LOWE PHOTO

A treasure supposedly lies hidden beneath the floors of Tumacácori National Monument.

gold bars from a mine near Gillette, a former mining camp that is now reduced to dust and rubble. Each bar measured three feet long by four inches wide. On today's market, they'd be worth a fortune that would make an oil baron smack his lips. They buried the bars near a cabin on Rogers Lake then hustled back into Flagstaff, where they robbed a stagecoach of an estimated twenty-five thousand dollars in gold and silver coins. They returned to their cabin, dug up the gold bars, and placed them, along with the strongbox from the stagecoach, into large wooden kegs. They then chopped holes into the ice covering Rogers Lake and lowered their loot into the freezing water.

The sheriff of Coconino County soon got word that the pair was holed up at the lake and organized a posse to bring them in. The robbers got wind of the plan, however, and left their hideout in a hurry. Unfortunately for them, the lake was still frozen over.

They didn't have time to retrieve their ill-gotten wealth, so they left it there. One outlaw was later killed in a gambling dispute and the other was arrested during a botched holdup and sentenced to prison, where he spent the next twenty-four years. After serving his time, he and an associate returned to Rogers Lake but never found the loot. Neither has anyone else, even though the lake goes almost dry every year, allowing the lake bed to be searched without major difficulty.

The emigrants and prospectors who passed through the Sonoran Desert near Gila Bend encountered a hostile land populated by hostile people. Those settlers who carved out their ranches and farms in the area were often subject to attack by the native peoples. One such attack occurred in 1869 and led to the discovery of a fabulously rich deposit of gold-bearing quartz in the Gila Bend Mountains. Apache raiders kidnapped a rancher's daughter, and several army troopers were sent out to search for her. One group of three soldiers didn't find the abducted girl, but they did stumble across a water hole filled with nuggets of pure gold. Directly above the depression, they also found two gold-bearing veins, one five inches across and the other sixteen inches wide.

The troopers filled their saddlebags with gold and set out to find their way back to their quarters, but they were forced to separate when their water ran out. One died there on the parched desert. The second made it back to civilization, but the experience left him so mentally disabled that no one ever believed his story. The third soldier, however, a private, got back with his saddlebags full of gold. After his discharge from the army, he mounted several expeditions into the mountains, but none ever found the pool of gold. In 1881, however, his body was found in the desert in Yuma County. He had his saddlebags with him and, according to the legend, they were filled with gold nuggets.

And so, before they rush out to buy pickaxes, burros, and floppy old hats, prospective prospectors should be aware that most, if not all, of these stories are sketchy, at best. They're based on fables, tall tales, campfire stories, and pure fiction.

But the legends go on and on.

And so do the searches.

WILLCOX: WHERE THE LEGENDS GROW OLD BUT NEVER DIE

On the surface, Willcox appears to be one of those nice, quiet little places where life carries on without much deviation from the norm. Located in Cochise County, it was founded in 1880 as a whistle stop on the Southern Pacific Railroad. Originally called Maley, it acquired the current name in 1889 in honor of Gen. Orlando B. Willcox, who rode in on the first train to arrive in the community.

The 2010 census set its population at 3,757. The Willcox High School athletic teams are called the Cowboys. In the early 1900s, the city was recognized as a national leader in cattle production.

Beneath that placid exterior, however, legends uncommon to such towns invite curiosity, and mysteries beg further examination. As a result, Willcox has gained both fame and notoriety as a place where such elements are dealt with as fact, fiction, speculation, and, perhaps, nothing out of the ordinary.

The legends are multiple. An Earp brother is buried there, primarily because he brought a knife to a gunfight. Another local character was even less prepared when he stormed into a shootout without his gun. He's buried outside of town. But the remains of a famous horse were interred in a city park.

One early Willcox resident got his start as a turkey herder. The city's favorite son was a cross-eyed guitar plucker, and the citizenry was once kept safe from bad guys by a lawman who moonlighted as a train robber.

The Willcox Town Hall cost one dollar. And, although the census doesn't show it, there are some who believe that a large number of Willcox residents are ghosts who allegedly hang around the main drag.

Many of the legends are supported by history and fact. The mysteries and ghost stories are not always given credibility, of course. However, those who relate them swear to their authenticity.

And now, some details:

Warren Earp was the youngest Earp brother, and he gets little of the publicity generated by his older brothers, especially Wyatt. Warren was probably in Tombstone on October 26, 1881, when the infamous gunfight at the OK Corral took place, but he was not involved. However, after Morgan Earp was assassinated and brother Virgil was badly wounded, Wyatt enlisted the services of his youngest sibling to go after the alleged culprits. The vendetta resulted in at least five deaths and warrants were issued for the Earps and three associates, but they fled to Colorado before facing any criminal action.

Warren returned to Arizona in 1891 and found work as a stage driver, then as a range detective for the Sierra Bonita Ranch, a huge spread owned by Henry Clay Hooker just outside of Willcox. He also developed a reputation as a bully because of his brothers' reputation. On July 6, 1900, he got into a verbal confrontation with Johnny Boyette, the Sierra Bonita range boss, in the Headquarters Saloon in downtown Willcox. The dispute escalated until Warren allegedly challenged Boyette to a gunfight. Boyette acquired two guns and fired off four rounds, probably meant as warnings. When Earp kept walking toward him, Boyette blasted him with a fifth and fatal shot. He claimed self-defense, even though Warren Earp was armed only with a small pocketknife that was discovered by the coroner after the incident.

Rumors began immediately afterwards that brothers Virgil and Wyatt stormed into town and killed Boyette, but that never happened. Boyette was arrested and charged, but he was acquitted and returned to ranching life.

Although the other Earp brothers were portrayed by such Hollywood luminaries as Henry Fonda, Kevin Costner, Burt Lancaster, Kurt Russell, Ward Bond, and Tim Holt, Warren made only one screen appearance. In the 1994 film *Wyatt Earp*, he was played by Jim Caviezel.

Despite that, his legacy lives on in Willcox during Warren Earp Days, an annual convention for Western writers. A small plaque commemorates the shooting at the former saloon (now occupied by a winery), and a welded steel marker has been erected over his grave site in the Old Pioneer Cemetery just outside the city limits.

Henry Clay Hooker might never have arrived in the Willcox area had he not tried his luck as a turkey herder.

While still a young man, Hooker arrived in California in the 1860s and started a mercantile business that sold supplies and equipment to miners. He also drove cattle over the Sierra Madres to sell to prospectors in Nevada. His future was looking good until August 10, 1865, when a fire destroyed both his store and his residence. Left with only about a thousand dollars, Hooker remembered that the Nevada miners were always willing to pay high prices for fresh meat, so he invested all his cash in five hundred live turkeys at $1.50 each. Then he, a hired man, and two dogs began herding them over the Sierra Nevada to the Comstock Lode.

But the expedition almost turned into tragedy. As the group neared their destination, they were confronted with a steep cliff. The men and dogs stopped to consider their options; the turkeys did not. They took flight over the edge of the cliff, and Hooker figured they'd all be killed when they hit bottom. But instead of plunging to their deaths, the birds soared and landed safely in the valley below, where they were easily rounded up. They were driven into Carson City and sold for five dollars a head, producing a net profit of $1,750.

Using that amount as seed money, Hooker purchased land and cattle near Willcox, named his spread the Sierra Bonita, and eventually ran as many as 15,550 cows in his herd. He once hired Billy the Kid as a ranch hand and helped the Earps elude capture after their vendetta ride.

As a child, Rex Allen had little chance of ever become anybody's favorite son. He was born in 1920 and raised on a ranch just outside of Willcox, a scrawny little kid who could play the guitar. He was also cross-eyed. While still living in the area, Allen underwent two surgeries in an attempt to straighten his eyes. Neither was successful. In his autobiography entitled *My Life: Sunrise to Sunset*, he remembered the ordeal:

> I started learning how to play the fiddle then, too, enough to play a few tunes at a dance or something like that. But I truthfully didn't have any ambitions about show business at that time, mainly because of my eyes. The only cross-eyed guy I ever knew that made any money was Ben Turpin, a movie actor who played a cross-eyed comedian. I thought, "Well, maybe that's what I'll do. I'll just be a Ben Turpin." . . . I'd just have to get used to having a maverick left eye. I'd joke that I could see around a haystack but, closer to the truth is that when I bawled, the tears would roll down my back.

Fortunately for the millions who would later watch him save the Old West from black-hatted bad guys in the movies and on television, Allen had surgery to correct the problem shortly after his singing career took off in Chicago. Both Gene Autry and Roy Rogers heard him sing and urged the young Arizonan to try his luck with recording and in the movies. So Allen migrated to the West Coast. It was a smart move, one that turned him from a small-town guitar strummer into a Western legend.

Eventually, Allen made it big. His records were bestsellers and he appeared in nineteen films as a cowboy hero who, while astride his horse KoKo, brought justice and music to the Old West. When the demand for the B Western movie subsided, then drifted completely away, Allen turned to television and starred in thirty-nine episodes of *Frontier Doctor*. When that role ended, he did narrations for Walt Disney films and voice-overs for TV commercials.

But he never forgot his hometown. He showed up at least once a year during Rex Allen Days and several other times just to sit and shoot the bull. And his hometown hasn't forgotten him in the years after his death in 1999. A larger-than-life bronze sculpture of his likeness gazes at the Rex Allen Museum directly across the street, and one of the city's major thoroughfares is named Rex Allen Drive. The remains of KoKo the horse are buried in the park near the statue, and Allen's ashes were scattered in the same area.

And a plaque next to the statue mentions the fact that he was once cross-eyed.

SAM LOWE PHOTO

Willcox's favorite son, Rex Allen, is immortalized in bronze in a downtown park.

Rex Allen's horse KoKo was buried in a park in downtown Willcox.

Two doors down from the Rex Allen Museum, Juanita Buckley tends to matters at the Friends of Marty Robbins Gift Shop and Museum. It was originally located in Glendale, Arizona, but she moved it to Willcox because, according to one popular (but unsubstantiated) legend, one of the cowboy singer's better-known ballads had Willcox roots.

The song, entitled "Big Iron," deals with a fatal showdown between Texas Red, a notorious gunslinger, and an unnamed Arizona Ranger. According to the lyrics, the ranger came to Agua Fria, a former community that butted up against Willcox, looking to capture Texas Red, alive or dead. Texas Red heard about the ranger's threat but wasn't worried because twenty men had tried to take him and they were all dead, and "twenty-one would be the ranger with the big iron on his hip."

In the song, the two met on the main street at a quarter past eleven, stared each other down, and then drew. The swiftness of the ranger, so the song goes, "is still talked about today," because Texas Red never even got his gun out of the holster before a bullet ended his miserable existence.

After hearing about the incident during one of his visits to Willcox, so the story goes, Robbins wrote and recorded the song in 1959. His version reached Number 26 on a 1960 Billboard chart and it's still selling in Willcox because it's supposed to be sort of true. And, although Willcox historians say it's pure fiction based on a rumor started by a couple of locals, the legend persists.

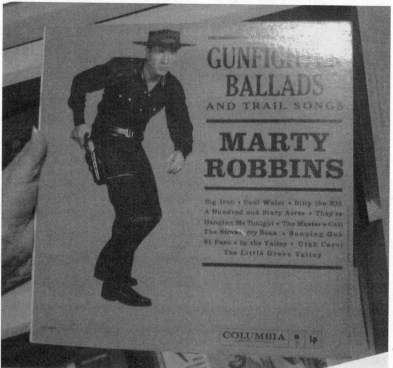

According to local lore, singer Marty Robbins wrote and recorded a song about a famous Willcox shootout.

In actuality, there was a well-documented shootout in the area between a bad guy named Bill Downing and a ranger named Billy Speed. Downing owned a saloon in Willcox, was blamed for as many as thirty deaths, and was known throughout the territory for his rotten disposition. Speed, the resident ranger, was ordered to put an end to Downing's nastiness by peaceful means or, if that failed, through use of force which, back in those days, usually meant a confrontation involving six-shooters.

On the fateful day, August 5, 1908, Downing was supposed to appear in court to settle a complaint filed against him. As he left his place of business, a friend advised him to leave his gun at home in order to stay out of trouble. So Downing left his gun on the bar and walked into the street, where he encountered Billy Speed. The ranger ordered him to raise his hands and Downing complied at first, but then reached for the pistol he usually carried. Unfortunately for him, it was the pistol he had left back on the bar. Speed didn't hesitate. He fired one shot but it was from his rifle, not a "big iron" as the song suggests. Either way, his aim was deadly and Downing's reign of terror was over.

Nobody missed him. Speed's supervisor noted: "This is the first time I have known a dead man to be without a single friend and the first time that I have known a killing to meet with absolute general rejoicing."

Another ranger echoed the sentiment: "Bill Downing was one of the most universally disliked desperadoes in southern Arizona. He bullied men and beat up women. Even his fellow outlaws couldn't stand him."

Southwest Studies Archives

Notorious Bill Downing was shot and killed by an Arizona Ranger.

Before all that happened, Downing had been an associate of Burt Alvord, the train-robbing lawman. Alvord had knocked around the territory for years, serving as a deputy under such high-powered sheriffs as Texas John Slaughter. But after his drinking problem cost him several jobs on one side of the law, he moved to the other side.

While employed as a constable in Willcox, Alvord rounded up a few ne'er-do-wells and formulated a method of robbing trains without getting caught. They'd do the crimes; he'd provide them with alibis. The first robbery occurred on September 11, 1899.

Alvord and four of his cronies took up temporary residence behind closed doors in the back room of Schwertner's Saloon in downtown Willcox and began playing poker. They bribed the bartender to bring them regular rounds, and then had him emerge from the room with empty glasses.

But while the barkeep came and went, only Alvord and one other player stayed in the room while some of the others slipped out a side window into the darkness. They rode to nearby Cochise Station, held up the train, then hustled back to town with an estimated thirty thousand dollars in gold. They then reentered the back room and resumed the game.

Word of the robbery rapidly spread through Willcox, and Constable Burt Alvord was soon notified. Pretending to be shocked, he organized a posse primarily composed of his poker-playing pals. They headed off in hot pursuit of the robbers but, naturally, were unable to apprehend them. To make sure that nobody suspected, Alvord then took the gold to a secret hiding place and buried it. Assuming he had pulled off the perfect crime, he went back to his job of keeping the public safe from people like himself.

But a suspicious Wells Fargo detective began snooping around because he suspected Alvord, and figured out how the gang had pulled off the heist. He convinced the bartender that he'd better cooperate with his investigation, but before charges could be brought, his star witness got cold feet and left town. Without his testimony, authorities couldn't proceed, so the matter was dropped. But not for long.

Overly cocky and flushed with success, Alvord planned another robbery about six months later. This one didn't go well. As

Southwest Studies Archives

Lawman Burt Alvord moonlighted as a train robber until he was caught.

they entered the express car, they were met with a shotgun-armed guard who mortally wounded one of them. The would-be robbers rode off empty-handed then left their wounded partner beside the trail to die. When a legitimate posse caught up with the dying bandit, he not only confessed but implicated all the others. One of those named was Burt Alvord. The people of Willcox had to find a new constable.

Alvord eventually served a term in Yuma Territorial Prison, but the whereabouts of the thirty thousand dollars in gold remains a mystery. However, stories still float around the area that after his release from prison, he somehow acquired enough money to buy a ranch in Central America.

The legend behind the Willcox Town Hall also involved a lot of money, but in this instance, it was all legitimate.

The actual cost of the building was one dollar. When the offer was made, most residents of Willcox figured there wouldn't be much trouble coming up with the necessary amount. Several of them even graciously offered to pay the entire sum all by themselves. But there was a hitch: The structure had to be moved.

The building was the old Southern Pacific Railroad depot, built in 1880 and the only remaining original redwood-frame station in Arizona. The depot was threatened with demolition when passenger service was discontinued but, after a public outcry of dissent and protest, the railroad offered to sell it to the city for a dollar. However, the sale included the stipulation that it had to be moved to a nearby piece of land. The railroad owned that land, and the railroad wanted eighteen thousand dollars for the property. All that, plus the cost of moving the building, elevated the total required funding to a figure that contained the word "thousands" and several zeroes. Plus the original one dollar.

Using donations and grants, the citizenry got the job done. They raised more than forty thousand dollars and the old depot was purchased, moved, and reopened as the new Town Hall on September 16, 1998. The relocated old depot still sits close to the railroad tracks, but now the trains whiz by with no intention of stopping. Most of the interior is used for city business, and the lobby is a mini-museum that spotlights scenes from the city's past.

The Willcox City Hall was formerly a railroad depot that cost the city one dollar.

The legend of the "Mirage of Willcox" was not a mirage. It was a seaplane that landed in the bone-dry desert.

On March 28, 1944, a twin-engine Martin PBM Mariner seaplane left Baltimore, headed for San Diego with a crew of six and a cargo of military supplies. But just east of El Paso, the flying machine developed an oil leak that caused one engine to shut down. The pilot, Lt. Scott Fitzgerald, realized the plane would never make it to San Diego in its current condition, so he looked for a body of water large enough to allow a seaplane landing.

The navigator found a dry lake bed near Willcox on a map, and the pilot decided it was their only chance. He eased the PBM down to about ten feet off the ground and raised the nose slightly, then set the plane adrift in a sea of sand. The craft touched down "so gently," Fitzgerald said later, "it felt as if you were drawing your fingers through sand."

One of the floats got knocked off, but there was little other damage to either the plane or its crew. A team from California repaired the oil leak, jacked the plane up, and installed wheels and modified beaching gear while the crew painted "The Mirage of Willcox" on the left side of the cockpit. Then, on May 28, the huge craft took off and completed its journey.

The days of yesteryear and the people who lived in them are also prominent factors in the Willcox ghost situation. The spirits of those who lived there long ago are still hanging around, according to those who believe in such things. Fortunately for those who reside there now, these are kind and friendly ghosts with no intent to do harm.

Both Rex Allen (1920–1999) and Marty Robbins (1925–1982) maintain a relationship with the community, according to the believers. Gayle Caulton, a volunteer at the Allen museum, turns off the recorded music and closes the doors every day in the late afternoon. But, she claims, she frequently gets calls from neighboring shops that the music has suddenly begun playing. After returning to the site, she shuts it down again, but by the time she gets home, it has started again. She thinks it's Rex.

Her contention is supported by Juanita Buckley at the Marty Robbins Gift Shop and Museum two doors down. She is among those who have called about the music emanating from the Allen facility. Not only that, she also feels a Robbins presence in her own establishment. And, she said, others also feel it. Raymon Grace, a well-known dowser and author, once called after visiting her establishment to tell her that both Marty and his grandfather were present. The grandfather, he said, followed him back to Virginia, but Marty's spirit still dwells in Willcox.

The ghost of Mr. Morton allegedly roamed around inside the old Commercial Building for years after his death. Believers said he was looking for his eyeglasses. When an employee found a pair of spectacles and placed them in a glass case inside the store, the apparitions stopped. Or so the story goes.

Henry Butcher was a drifter who was shot and killed while riding into Willcox in 1888. Those who follow such cases say his ghost is still drifting around in front of the Rex Allen statue, and that he will appear to those who stand in front of the sculpture and yell, "Show yourself, Henry Butcher!" Actual sightings are rare. But, say the believers, that doesn't mean they don't occur.

BUCKEY O'NEILL:
A HERO IN LIFE,
A LEGEND IN DEATH

On the morning of July 3, 1907, a parade featuring cavalry, a marching band, a troop of Spanish-American War veterans, a few Civil War veterans, the territorial governor, and a variety of other dignitaries came to a halt in front of a large drapery hanging over a tall sculpture on the north lawn of the Yavapai County Courthouse in Prescott, Arizona. There, a crowd estimated at more than seven thousand gathered to watch as the cloth was removed to reveal a magnificent bronze statue.

It was a larger-than-life depiction of a man astride a horse. The sculptor didn't specifically name the man, but to those present, there was no doubt about the person represented. It was William Owen O'Neill, even though nobody called him that. To them, he was Buckey O'Neill, and he was their hero. A fallen hero revered by almost every Arizonan at the time. A hero whose death elevated him to immortality.

The historical accounts of the day's activities noted that as the speakers extolled the virtues of the hometown patriot, tears filled the eyes of many of those who had known him in days gone by, and who had been proud to call him friend. A great pity welled up in the hearts of the rugged, honest, God-fearing Arizonans that he was not still with them in the flesh. And with bared heads, while the band played "America," those present paid homage to the memory of the brave Buckey O'Neill.

Long before the term "renaissance man" became commonplace, Buckey O'Neill was a renaissance man. He was, at various times, a lawman, politician, miner, court reporter, school principal, tax assessor, land developer, construction worker, newspaper reporter and publisher, soldier, lobbyist, and gambler. His nickname reflected that latter occupation; he came by it due to his propensity for betting against the house in the game of faro, a practice known as "bucking the tiger." He was successful and popular during his lifetime, then became a legend after his death at age thirty-eight while fighting with Teddy Roosevelt in the Spanish-American War.

O'Neill was born in St. Louis in 1860 and migrated to the West while in his teens. He got one of his first tastes of adventure in early 1882 while serving as a special deputy for the city of Phoenix. One summer night, three drunken cowboys began shooting up a downtown street. O'Neill and three other lawmen tried to arrest them, but the trio mounted their horses and raced toward the policemen with guns blazing. Henry Garfias, the city marshal, fired two shots at the leader. One knocked the gun from his hand; the second was fatal. The other two surrendered immediately.

A short time later, O'Neill arrived in Prescott, and it became his home for the remainder of his short life. He had already worked as a reporter for John Clum's *Tombstone Epitaph* in the early 1880s, and he stayed with the profession in Prescott by taking a reporter's job with the *Arizona Miner*, then founding his own newspaper, a livestock publication entitled *Hoof and Horn*. After that, he joined the Prescott Volunteer Fire Department and was on the scene when the town's infamous Whiskey Row burned. He became captain of the local unit of the Arizona Militia in 1886 and, much to his embarrassment, once fainted while the unit stood guard at a hanging.

His handsome face and devil-may-care attitude attracted many of Prescott's eligible young women, but he settled the issue on April 27, 1886, by marrying Pauline Schindler. She bore him a son but he died in infancy, so they adopted a four-year-old boy and named him Maurice. Buckey's multifaceted lifestyle went on unimpeded. He was elected Yavapai County judge, then county sheriff in 1888. It was in that capacity that he earned much of the admiration that was to follow.

On March 20, 1889, four masked men robbed the Atlantic and Pacific Railroad passenger train at Canyon Diablo and made off with about seven thousand dollars before heading north on a trail that would lead them across the Navajo Reservation toward Utah. At that time, Yavapai County covered all of northern Arizona, and Prescott was more than a hundred miles from the site of the holdup. But, although he had been in office for only a short time, O'Neill recognized his sworn duty, organized a three-man posse, and set out in pursuit.

The posse sent telegraph messages alerting towns along the Utah border to be on the lookout for the robbers, who had already terrorized the small community of Cannonville. The outlaws then circled back on their own trail near Lees Ferry along the Colorado River in an effort to confuse the posse, but O'Neill and his men weren't fooled. They picked up the trail and found the bandits' camp. O'Neill raced ahead and was met by gunfire. One bullet knocked his horse down and he was pinned underneath, but the rest of the posse arrived, pried him loose, and the chase resumed. Because all the commotion spooked the bandits' horses, it wasn't long before the sore-footed quartet was taken into custody.

The adventure lasted almost three weeks, and the posse covered more than six hundred miles. After it was over, an area judge wrote that "Yavapai County's young sheriff with his rough riders . . . has scarcely a parallel for daring and pertinacity in this or any other county."

The judge's use of "rough riders" would eventually prove prophetic.

Many years later, after the robbers served their respective sentences in Yuma Territorial Prison, and after O'Neill's untimely death, a rumor began circulating that claimed William Sterin, one of the outlaws, changed his name, joined the Rough Riders, and was killed in Cuba. It was a popular theory, but the allegation was never substantiated.

After his term as sheriff ended, O'Neill was unanimously elected mayor of Prescott. But, still young and ambitious, he joined the Populist Party and ran for delegate to the United States House of Representatives in 1894 and 1896. He lost both times; however, he kept getting reelected mayor. In that capacity, he worked tirelessly to keep the territorial capital in Prescott. The city held that distinction from 1864 through 1867, but lost out to Tucson for a ten-year stretch that lasted until 1877, when it was returned to

Prescott. The "roaming capital" issue was settled for good in 1889, when it moved to Phoenix, where it remains.

Between political campaigns, lobbying for Arizona statehood, and tending to his mayoral duties, O'Neill turned to copper mining and railroad development at the Grand Canyon. He found a copper deposit but realized that shipping costs would eat up all his profits, so he quit prospecting and built two structures at the canyon: a cabin that he used as an office and an adjacent bunkhouse. He combined all those activities with a lobbying effort aimed at creating a railroad spur that would run from Williams to the canyon.

In 1897 O'Neill finally convinced local business owners to fund the Santa Fe and Grand Canyon Railroad Company, and he was named its president. But construction didn't start until two years after his death. When the original company went bankrupt, the Santa Fe Railway bought it and finished laying track in 1901. Today, a tourist train makes regular runs between Williams and the Grand Canyon on those same tracks.

His cabin, located on the Bright Angel Trail, also followed him into history. In 1935 Mary Jane Colter, an architect for the Fred Harvey Company, remodeled it and converted it into guest quarters. It then became part of a two-million-dollar renovation project in 2007.

None of those outside endeavors hurt O'Neill's standing among the citizenry of Prescott, because they kept reelecting him as their mayor. He was the city's top executive in 1898 when the Spanish-American War broke out after the battleship USS *Maine* was sunk in Havana Harbor.

And Buckey O'Neill's path in life was about to take a fateful turn.

As the battle cry of "Remember the *Maine!*" fueled the war fervor, O'Neill began recruiting men from all over the Southwest who expressed a desire to join the fight. When Theodore Roosevelt resigned as assistant secretary of the navy and received permission to raise a volunteer cavalry, he formed the First Volunteer Cavalry Regiment, which included O'Neill and his mixed assortment of cowboys, miners, and trappers, selected because they were the first to offer their services to the war effort. O'Neill was soon named a captain and assigned to command Company A. He tried to recruit an entire regiment of Arizona cowboys, but the effort failed. Eventually only three troops were authorized.

Under the leadership of Roosevelt and Alexander Brodie, the regiment commander, the volunteers became a crack fighting outfit and earned the nickname the Rough Riders after Roosevelt remarked to a newspaper reporter that he was joining "a regiment of rough riding men." Buckey O'Neill soon became its most popular officer. His noble sense of justice earned him the unqualified admiration of his charges, as well as the respect of his fellow officers, most notably that of Teddy Roosevelt.

After a brief training period in San Antonio, Texas, the Rough Riders were sent to Tampa, Florida, the final staging area before shipping out to Cuba. Once there, the men were informed that there wasn't room for all of them on the transports, so several were left behind—so were their horses, for the same reason. But Roosevelt, fully aware that a cavalry without horses isn't much of a cavalry, commandeered a transport to carry the mounts to the war zone.

O'Neill's bravery in the face of danger was almost immediate. As the Rough Riders were landing in Daiquiri, Cuba, on June 22, 1898, two members of the Tenth Cavalry's famed Buffalo Soldiers fell overboard due to the rough seas. Although in full uniform, O'Neill jumped into the water and tried to rescue the pair, but his efforts were in vain.

Once the Rough Riders were in place as a fighting force in Cuba, O'Neill resumed his position as his unit's most popular officer and a favorite of the press corps assigned to cover the war. In combat, he firmly believed that his place was in front of his men rather than hunkered down in the trenches. "An officer should never take cover," he said frequently, and he would live by those words over the course of the next seven days. During every skirmish, he defied Spanish marksmen while walking up and down the lines in front of his troops, setting an example to bolster their courage.

He continued to defy death in the same manner but, although it fit his persona, it also led to his demise. A Spanish bullet did find him.

Accounts of his final moments vary, but some elements were certain. It happened on July 1, 1898. The Rough Riders were deployed to San Juan Heights and positioned at the base of Kettle Hill, where they faced a barrage of enemy fire. True to his nature, O'Neill strode up and down the line, calming those in his command, when a single bullet struck him in the mouth. He died instantly. Some said O'Neill had turned toward the Spanish lines, rolling another cigarette while stubbornly ignoring suggestions and pleas that he take cover, when the fatal missile hit. Others said he

Buckey O'Neill's life came to an end during the Spanish-American War.

was chatting with his men when a Mauser slug found its target. Regardless of which version was the most accurate, Buckey's life had come to an end.

The men of Company A, although shocked by the sudden death of their beloved commander, rallied around Roosevelt as he led the troops up the slopes of Kettle Hill in the face of withering fire. Assisted by regiments of the Buffalo Soldiers, they seized that target, and then launched an assault across open ground to rout the Spanish from their posts on San Juan Hill. Two days later, the Spanish fleet was destroyed while attempting to break through the US naval blockade, literally ending the war.

Theodore Roosevelt later wrote about O'Neill's death:

The most serious loss that I and the regiment could have suffered befell just before we charged. O'Neill was strolling up and down in front of his men, smoking his cigarette, for he was inveterately addicted to the habit. He had the theory that an officer ought never take cover—a theory which was, of course, wrong, though in a volunteer organization the officers should certainly expose themselves very fully, simply for the effect on the men. . . . As O'Neill moved to and fro, his men begged him to lie down, and one of the sergeants said, "Captain, a bullet is sure to hit you." O'Neill took his cigarette out of his mouth and blowing out a cloud of smoke laughed and said, "Sergeant, the Spanish bullet isn't made that will kill me.". . . As he turned on his heel, a bullet struck him in the mouth and came out the back of his head; so that even before he fell his wild and gallant soul had gone out into the darkness.

O'Neill was originally buried in Cuba, but in 1899 Rev. Henry A. Brown, the Rough Rider chaplain, went back to retrieve the body, which was returned to the United States and reinterred in Arlington National Cemetery. His tomb bears the words he had once written: "Who would not die for a new star on the flag," an apparent reference to his struggle to gain statehood for Arizona.

Prescott mourned the loss, and the city fathers immediately began formulating plans for a memorial. And the story of the memorial is equally interesting.

The city commissioned Solon Borglum, who began working on a sculpture in 1905. Borglum, the younger brother of Mount Rushmore's sculptor, Gutzon Borglum, poured himself into the creation of the statue. A newspaper reporter noted that "Borglum himself was part of the land that had . . . drawn the men of the Rough Riders together to give their lives if need be for the freedom of a land and people far from their own Southwest. . . . And out of those fused fires came the greatest equestrian statue in the United States."

Some of Solon Borglum's other works are still on display in galleries and museums in such major cities as Paris, St. Louis, Atlanta, San Francisco, New York, and Portland, Oregon. He died in 1922, long before his brother undertook his most memorable work in the Black Hills of South Dakota.

Although the artist was dedicated, completion of the project was not without complications. The statue sits atop a twenty-eight-ton boulder, and getting that in place was a major drawback. After the giant rock was blasted out of the neighboring mountains, somebody had to haul it into Prescott and emplace it on the right spot in front of the courthouse. In the words of the local newspaper, "Many weary days were spent by contractor H. C. Walter and his men, in transporting the boulder to its present resting place. It was tedious work, owning to the cumberousness of the granite rock, but no work was too tedious for those who knew to what purpose the stone was to be put. Finally, it was embedded on a cement foundation in the city plaza, and all was in readiness for the mounting of the statue, which at that time had not yet arrived."

The statue had not yet arrived because there were troubles.

Borglum built it in New York, and it was scheduled to be shipped by rail to Prescott in plenty of time for the dedication ceremony. But there were problems along the route, and it took intervention by a railroad vice president to get it there on time.

The newspaper described the episode in this manner: "Grave fears were entertained that it would not arrive in time for the unveiling ceremonies . . . then it was demonstrated that railroads are not always the 'soulless corporations' the muck-rakers like to picture them, and that a thread of sentiment, even like that which runs through the beings of everyday mortals, is present also in the make-up of railroad systems."

Once made aware of the situation, Santa Fe Railway vice president W. A. Drake appointed agent H. G. Wells to dispatch a special train to look for the sculpture and rush it to Prescott. Wells was "given the power to spare neither time nor expense in securing trace of the statue and getting it here on time." He found it in an Albuquerque railroad yard, ordered it out on the first train leaving the city, then got on board to make sure all went well on the final leg of the journey.

All didn't go well.

It's the Buckey O'Neill Memorial to most as it sits in front of the Yavapai County Court House in Prescott.

Shortly after crossing into Arizona Territory, the car carrying the statue broke down at Winslow. So the train was held up for several hours while all available mechanics were brought in to make the necessary repairs. When the train reached Ash Fork, several miles north of Prescott, a special engine was waiting to take the car and the statue to the final destination. They got there only days before the unveiling. The task of mounting the work on the granite pedestal took another two days, and the ceremony went on as scheduled.

Buckey's adopted son, Maurice, and Kate Hickey, daughter of one of his closest friends, were delegated to do the actual unveiling. And the newspaper's account proclaimed, "With impressive ceremonies, the draperies were pulled aside from Borglum's beautiful statue, revealing the gallant captain, mounted on his charger. With distended nostrils the horse stands slightly reared back on his haunches as though abruptly pulled up, while his rider, with face turned toward the left, sits in an attitude of expectancy, as though awaiting orders."

Technically, however, the sculpture is not a statue of Buckey O'Neill. Borglum designed and created it as a tribute to the Rough Riders. But O'Neill being the hometown hero that he was, the local citizens have come to associate it with him. So in Prescott, it's the Buckey O'Neill Monument—the same today as it was on July 3, 1907.

BIBLIOGRAPHY

Ira Hayes: Arizona's Reluctant Hero

Bradley, James, and Ron Powers. *Flags of Our Fathers*. New York: Bantam Books, 2000.

Fey, Harold, and D'Arcy McNickle. *Indians and Other Americans*. New York: Perennial Library, 1970.

"Ira Hamilton Hayes, Corporal, United States Marine Corps." Arlington National Cemetery website. www.arlingtoncemetery .net/ irahayes.htm.

Lowe, Sam. "Battle of Ira Hayes." *Arizona Republic*, February 23, 1998.

Trimble, Marshall. *Arizona 2000: A Yearbook for the Millennium*. Flagstaff, AZ: Northland Publishing, 1998.

Abby Still Lives in the Hotel Vendome

Christensen, Jo-Anne. *Haunted Hotels*. Auburn, WA: Ghost House Books, 2002.

Eppinga, Jane. *Arizona Twilight Tales*. Boulder, CO: Pruett Publishing Company, 2000.

Mulford, Karen Surina. *Arizona's Historic Escapes*. Winston-Salem, NC: John F. Blair, Publisher, 1997.

Cecil Creswell: Arizona's Lady Rustler

Brisendine, James. "The Cecil Creswell Story." 1954. Old Trails Museum, Winslow, AZ.

Cameron, Bill. "Suicide of 'Cecil' Ends One of the Strangest Stories in the Colorful History of the County." *Winslow Mail*, March 12, 1954.

Thomas, Bob. "Cecil Cresswell." *Arizona Highways*, October 1995.

James Addison Reavis: The Man Who Conned Arizona

Adams, John. "The Man Who Called Himself 'Baron.'" *The Downey Eagle*, December 6, 1996.

Cook, James. *Arizona Trivia*. Baldwin Park, CA: Gem Guides Book Company, 1991.

Cookridge, E. H. *The Baron of Arizona*. New York: John Day Company, 1967.

Kollenborn, Tom. "The Baron of Arizona." *Apache Junction News*, July 7, 2008.

Myers, John. "The Prince of Swindlers." *American Heritage Magazine*, May 1956.

Trimble, Marshall. *In Old Arizona*. Phoenix, AZ: Golden West Publishers, 1985.

Apache Leap: Legend, Myth, or Fact?

Barney, James. "How Apache Leap Got Its Name." *Arizona Highways*, October 1940.

Cook, James. "The Haunting Legend of Apache Leap." *Arizona Highways*, June 1977.

Jarman, Max. "Mine Pushes Land Swap for Oak Flats and Apache Leap National Recreation Area." *Arizona Republic*, May 9, 2009.

Lake, Ted. "Apache Leap." *Copper Country News*, May 30, 2009.

Scott, C. S. "The Story of Apache Leap." *Arizona Magazine*, October, 1914.

Superior Chamber of Commerce. "Legends of Apache Leap and Apache Tears." Informational brochure updated annually.

Pearl Hart: The Last Stagecoach Robber

Anderson, Parker. "How a Woman Stagecoach Robber Became a Famous Outlaw." Sharlot Hall Museum Days Past Archives, July 26, 2002.

Matas, Kimberly. "Pearl Hart, Smooth-Talking Card Shark Led to Pearl's Slide to Perdition." *Arizona Daily Star*, October 31, 2008.

New York Times. "Pearl Hart Acquitted." November 17, 1899.

Thompson, Clay. "Bandita Drove Stage Robberies Into History." *Arizona Republic*, May 26, 2008.

Trimble, Marshall. *Arizona 2000: A Yearbook for the Millennium.* Flagstaff, AZ: Northland Publishing, 1998.

The Red Ghost: Fictionalized Fact or Factual Fiction?

Berg, Robert. "Camels West." *Saudi Aramco World*, May/June 2002.

Froman, Robert. "The Red Ghost." *American Heritage Magazine*, April 1961.

Lowe, Sam. "Camel Driver's Dream Lives On in Quartzsite." *Arizona Republic*, December 14, 1999.

Thompson, Clay. "Arizona Hunters Would Walk More Than a Mile for a Camel." *Arizona Republic*, November 26, 2007.

Trimble, Marshall. "The Legend of the Red Ghost." Lecture delivered to students at Scottsdale Community College, Scottsdale, AZ, 1988 to present.

Teresa Urrea: The Woman Who Healed

Goliath Business News. "From Saint to Seeker: Teresa Urrea's Search for a Place of Her Own." September 1, 2006.

L'abeille de la Nouvelle Orleans. "Santa Teresa Heard From." January 29, 1898.

Lowe, Sam. "Saint Preserve Us." *Arizona Republic*, March 25, 1996.

New York Times. "A Saint to Be Shot." June 16, 1892.

Urrea, Luis. *The Hummingbird's Daughter*. New York: Little, Brown and Company, 2005.

Mysterious Grand Canyon Deaths

Brady, Lee. "River of No Return." *Pacific Sun*, September 23, 2005.

The Charley Project. "Bessie Louise Haley Hyde" and "Glen Rollin Hyde." Cold case investigative series first posted October 12, 2004. Updated November 2008. www.charleyproject.org/cases/h/hyde_bessie.html and www.charleyproject.org/cases/h/hyde_glen.html.

Dimock, Brad. *Sunk Without a Sound: The Tragic Colorado River Honeymoon of Glen and Bessie Hyde*. Flagstaff, AZ: Fretwater Press, 2001.

Stanley, John. "Canyon Vanishing Act a Grand Mystery." *Arizona Republic*, March 31, 2008.

The Apache Kid: A Shadow in Arizona's History

Anderson, Guy, and Donna Anderson, eds. *Adventures and Disasters Marked the Lives of Lawmen*. Gila County Centennial Commission Production, 1975.

Bigando, Robert. *Globe, Arizona: The Life and Times of a Western Mining Town.* Globe, AZ: Mountain Spirit Press, 1989.

Haak, William. *Copper Bottom Tales: Historic Sketches from Gila County.* Globe, AZ: Gila County Historical Society, 1991.

Hurst, James. "The Apache Kid." *Desert USA Magazine,* November 1999.

Gabrielle Darley: Heartless Murderess or Innocent Victim?

Banks, Leo. "Unusual Deaths Followed Husbands of Famous Prescott Madam." *Sharlot Hall Museum Days Past,* January 20, 2002.

Ruland-Thorne, Kate. "Dial M For Murdering Madam." *Sedona Magazine,* Winter 2008/09.

Review of *The Red Kimona.* www.moviediva.com. From 1925.

_____. www.dvdtalk.com/silentdvd/first_ladies. From 1925.

Arizona's Lost Treasures: They're Still Waiting

Banks, Leo. "Golden Chimney of the Aravaipas." *Arizona Highways,* November 2004.

Christensen, Kerry. "Geronimo's Story of Hidden Gold." *Arizona Highways,* November 2004.

Lowe, Sam. "Ghost Gold of the Southwest." *Arizona Highways,* July 1980.

Schnell, Caramie. "John D. Lee: Secretive Polygamist." *National Geographic Adventure Magazine*, March 2004.

―――――. "The Legend of Frontier Jesuit Treasure." *Arizona Highways*, November 2004.

Willcox: Where the Legends Grow Old but Never Die

Allen, Rex. *My Life, Sunrise to Sunset*. Scottsdale, AZ, RexGarRus Press, 1989.

Clement, Howard. "The Mariner on the Lake." *Pacific Flyer*, May 1998.

Cochise County Office of Economic and Community Development. "Official Destination Guide of Cochise County." *Sierra Vista Herald*, 2012.

Cochise County Tourism Council. "Cochise County, Land of Legends." *Sierra Vista Herald*, 2008.

Lowe, Sam. *Arizona Curiosities*. 3rd ed. Guilford, CT: Globe Pequot Press, 2012.

Trimble, Marshall. *Arizona Outlaws and Lawmen*. Charleston, SC: History Press, 2015.

Buckey O'Neill: A Hero in Life, a Legend in Death

Heatwole, Thelma. *Ghost Towns and Historical Haunts in Arizona*. Phoenix, AZ: Golden West Publishers, 1991.

Naylor, Roger. "Buckey O'Neill and the Rough Riders." *Arizona Republic*, May 15, 2015.

Powell, Marian. "The Remarkable Story of Solon Borglum." Sharlot Hall Museum Library. Accessed December 1, 2015. www.sharlot.org/library-archives/days-past/the-remarkable-story-of-solon-borglum.

Trimble, Marshall. "Arizona's True Tales." *Arizona Republic*, August 1, 2015.

INDEX

ABOUT THE AUTHOR

Sam Lowe has lived in and been writing about Arizona for the past forty-five years. During that time, his stories have appeared in such publications as *Arizona Highways, Arizona Highroads, Robb Report, Arizona Republic, Phoenix Gazette, Phoenix Magazine, International Tours and Tourism News,* and the *Columbus Dispatch.* He has also written twelve books about the state, including *Speaking Ill of the Dead: Jerks in Arizona History, Arizona Curiosities,* and *You Know You're in Arizona When . . .* for Globe Pequot. In April 2009 he was named the Senior Travel Expert for Best Western International. Lowe lives in Phoenix with his wife, Lyn, and his dog, Zachary, both faithful and loyal companions.